Artisanal Theology

Artisanal Theology

Intentional Formation
in Radically Covenantal
Companionship

LISA M. HESS

CASCADE *Books* • Eugene, Oregon

ARTISANAL THEOLOGY
Intentional Formation in Radically Covenantal Companionship

Cascade Books
A Division of Wipf and Stock Publishers
199 W. 8th Ave., Suite 3
Eugene, OR 97401

www.wipfandstock.com

ISBN 13: 978-1-55635-875-3

Cataloging-in-Publication data:

Hess, Lisa M.

    Artisanal theology : intentional formation in radically covenantal companionship
/ Lisa M. Hess.

    xxii + 128 p. ; 23 cm. —Includes bibliographical references.

    ISBN 13: 978-1-55635-875-3

    1. Theology, Practical. 2. Theology—Study and teaching. 3. Pastoral Theology.
I. Title.

BV1464 .H47 2009

Manufactured in the U.S.A.

Excerpt from *The Human Condition* by Thomas Keating. Copyright © 1999 by St.
Benedict's Monastery, Snowmass, CO Paulist Press, Inc. New York/Mahwah, NJ.
Reprinted by permission of Paulist Press, Inc. www.paulistpress.com

Contents

Foreword

Mary Elizabeth Mullino Moore

Artisanal Theology is a book for artists and poets, for people who cook and people who feast. I delighted in reading this artisanal vision of theology and theological education, posed in terms associated with artistry and food. As one who loves to cook and eat, this stirs my imagination. As one who treasures the covenantal power of the common table, this challenges me to think more deeply and push theological and educational ideas more radically. True to Lisa Hess's own method, I will begin with stories and reflections upon them.

I remember teaching a doctoral seminar on the Wednesday before Thanksgiving and having the class go very badly. I remember how exhausted I was when I stopped at the grocery store and bought Thanksgiving groceries on the way home that day, wondering how I could possibly find the energy to make two pies and cornbread that night and begin other preparations for dinner the next day. I wondered how I could face Thanksgiving at all, feeling quite discouraged with myself and my teaching. Thanksgiving guests were coming, however, so I bought the groceries and began to "slug" my way through pie baking, re-living the terrible class session as I rolled the dough. An hour or so after I had forced myself into pie-baking, I realized that I was no longer thinking of the class as "the end of the world," but was feeling a bit lighter. I even had an insight or two about how the class could be moved in a more positive direction the following week. I began to relax and enjoy cooking, discovering the healing that comes when one engages raw ingredients with one's hands and creates something delicious.

I have had many such moments since this one. In fact, I often include cooking in my work, delighting in having groups of students in our home. Further, I often seek opportunities to cook when feeling a bit scattered or discouraged. My insight in the Thanksgiving experience has stayed with me. At the time I interpreted it as "re-connecting with the primal." Lisa Hess's association of such moments with radical covenantal community is not at all far-fetched. Such experiences with food connect people with the fruits of the earth, the senses of touch and smell and taste, the people with whom or for whom one prepares a meal, and the wisdom of the ages (grandmother's recipes, father's sauces, grandfather's stories, and memories of a sister's companionship).

To this Thanksgiving story, I add some snapshots of church communities living into radical covenantal community. I think of my cousin's Episcopal parish where a group of women gather every week to bake communion wafers from fresh ingredients. I think of Candler School of Theology's special communion bread, baked by a student each week. I particularly remember one of those bakers saying to me that she treasured the bread-baking; it relaxed and grounded her, helping her return to her center. I also think of Claremont School of Theology's graduation tradition of communion with diverse breads from across the world, offered to the table by people from those many places. I think too of a Native American congregation that, for years, offered Sunday dinner to homeless people in their community. The congregation prepared the meal and sat to enjoy the food with the homeless folk, making the distinction no longer visible to an outsider. Indeed, over time, the homeless people helped with the preparations as well.

To these pictures, I add other snapshots of people living in community with one another, communities that embody Hess's vivid communal visions. I think of the Orthodox Jews in our neighborhood who fill the streets on Friday evenings and Saturdays, walking comfortably together, often in lively or earnest conversation. The practices of their faith include a commitment to Sabbath simplicity—walking and refraining from work. They also include the joyful celebration of holy days with their families and community—Sabbath meals, Passover celebrations, Sukkot (booths) for the commemorative harvest festival, and so forth.

Most Christian bodies do not practice Sabbath in such simplified, communal ways; however, groups often do find ways to bind themselves in ever-deepening spiritual practice. I think of the Methodist Federation for Social Action, which gathers for the sake of collective action but which increasingly gives time for worship, storytelling, and communal sharing, building a covenantal community for the sake of building a deeper justice and peace. I think of my own adult Sunday school class, which we have named "Sabbath Seekers." We are an intergenerational group that shares the hardest, most challenging, and most joyful parts of our life journeys within a context of prayer and communal searching for wisdom. We choose a book or approach for several weeks, then we follow the course but without guilt. When we gather, some have read and some have not. It does not matter. We always spend time in silence, praying and meditating. We read scripture and other texts of the tradition. We sometimes journal, sometimes practice spiritual disciplines that are new or familiar to us, and sometimes discuss theological or existential concerns. We laugh and cry, write poetry, and tell stories. The food of this group is spiritual practice, which enables us to participate in Sabbath each week.

I have shared an array of stories and snapshots to give a sense of hope, but also to reveal some of colors and textures of artisanal theology and theological education. These stories also embody some of the defining characteristics of artisanal foods. They are: homemade, handcrafted from natural ingredients, personalized, simplified, local, and rich with taste.[1] Some observers have identified the growing interest in artisanal food as the Slow Food Movement because the growth, production, and sales are done in low-technology, local, and simplified ways.[2] Many people describe the trend as one that promises greater simplification of life overall, attuning the human community to what is most important for global ecology. One blogger, Joe, says: "I hope the artisanal movement grows in an authentic way, in concert with the relocalizing of our economies as fossil fuels dwindle, to help undo the excesses of industrialization."[3] Another blogger argues that the entire artisanal movement

1. One description of the artisanal movement includes ten defining characteristics: human scale, handmade, relatively raw and untransformed, unbranded, personalized, transparent, authentic, local, preference for a new connoisseurship (tasty but without pretence), and simplified. See: http://www.cultureby.com/trilogy/2006/11/the_artisanal_m.html (accessed 14 November 2008). These descriptors can be applied to cheeses, bread, olives, salt, chocolate, ice cream, and many other products. See also: http://www.portigal.com/blog/fruit-comes-to-the-door/ (accessed 14 November 2008).

2. Carol Ness, 2006. "Slow Food Movement has Global Outreach: Farmers, Producers Share Knowledge at Italy convention," *San Francisco Chronicle*, 30 October 2006. See: http://www.sfgate.com/cgi-bin/article.cgi?file=/c/a/2006/10/30/MNGBRM2HL51.DTL (accessed 14 November 2008).

3. Joe, blog entry, 17 January 2007. See: http://www.cultureby.com/trilogy/2006/11/

has "an underlying 'ethic of community.'"[4] Marty Olmstead describes the artisanal movement as "a remedy to the blandness of mechanization and industrial farming," and she describes the food artisans as people who "bring passion and personality to the products they grow, harvest, culture, and otherwise bring to our tables."[5] Still others emphasize the artistry of this artisanal movement, with its delight-filled preparations and delicious productions.[6]

These are descriptions of a popular movement, but they capture much of what Lisa Hess sketches as a theological vision, supported by her theological and social-scientific analysis. Stories and descriptors of the artisanal rebirth portray a movement that connects people with basic human functions (such as food preparation), with natural products in local areas, with small communities of production and consumption, and with simpler, healthier lifestyles. This movement does not necessarily lead to less work, but it will definitely lead to more grounded, more basic work. It will also lead to more personal contact with others involved in the movement or in the local food chain.

The descriptors also point to possibilities for theological and ministerial formation that Hess has developed helpfully in her book. I will accent some of those possibilities here. What would theology look like if those of us who claim to be professional theologians spent part of every week engaging in theological discourse with local communities? How would theologians reshape their ideas if they regularly engaged with public issues in local public media and in the halls of legislatures and social agencies? How would theological educators reshape their institutions if they planned for every student to engage with a local community over time and to participate with that community in food gathering, food preparations, neighborhood clean-ups, or other basic human functions? What shape might theological education take if those same students reflected with the communities on God and the world and the God-world

---

the_artisanal_m.html (accessed 14 November 2008).

4. Tommy Stinson, blog entry, 9 November 2006. See: http://www.cultureby.com/trilogy/2006/11/the_artisanal_m.html (accessed 14 November 2008).

5. See: Olmstead, "Artisanal Food Producers and Fruits of Their Labor," in http://www.winecountry.com/winecountry_publication/archive/2005/03/feature_article/index.html (accessed 14 November 2008).

6. Terrance Brennan and Andrew Friedman, *Artisanal Cooking: A Chef Shares His Passion for Handcrafting Great Meals at Home* (Hoboken, NJ: Wiley, 2005).

relationship? Many contextual education programs do move in this direction, but the fullness of such engagement is rarely included in theological education.

Another accent of this work is the practice of spiritual disciplines, which is a growing concern of theological schools. Schools in the past twenty years have increasingly included spiritual growth groups, mini-courses and groups focused on prayer, and so forth; however, most theological schools decry their own lack of sustained and edifying attention to spiritual practices. Even Roman Catholic seminaries have expressed this concern, though they have generally maintained such practices in their weekly patterns, allowing them to languish less than in Protestant schools.

Where does this discussion lead? I suggest that it leads to six emphases for theology and theological education in the future, all designed to enhance wisdom: opportunities for practicing spiritual disciplines and deepening relationships with God; spiritual direction offered individually and/or in small groups; opportunities for social-theological engagement with texts of tradition and with local communities; participation in the human arts of basic living (growing food, cooking, cleaning, making music, crafting implements, and so forth); engagement with local groups addressing global issues; and theological reflection and construction in relation to these diverse activities with local folk. From such a grounded approach to theology, theological schools and other educational institutions and communities could enhance the "house of living stones" about which we read in 1 Peter 2:1–5. A house of living stones is not built from pre-fabricated bricks made on an assembly line, but it is handcrafted from the lives of passionate human beings who are willing to participate in a living, changing, and hope-filled community.

Mary Elizabeth Mullino Moore

Acknowledgments

To the companions who lived through this work, in all its lived and written forms, I offer a relieved, impish smile and a sense of deep gratitude. John Paddock and Robert Walker were both generous with their time and wisdom, getting the writing off the ground with their persistent questions and expressed faith in me. My colleague and friend Gary Eubank read more drafts than were ever in his job description to read. An unexpected and holy-serendipitous companion, Irwin Kula, startled me into new awareness and courage about what has been given here to say. I am thankful for our friendship and for what we are receiving, even as we learn and live it forward. I am thankful to United Theological Seminary, which granted the sabbatical time and offered the coverage for the work to develop into its final forms for the students who enter into MIN groups each year. Thanks also to Lisa Withrow, who sketched the path of progress when I hadn't the least idea how to proceed. Editor Charlie Collier and Cascade Books made this project possible. The company's origin, history and faithful contributions to the publishing world offered such immediate resonance with the thrust of this project, the choice of collaboration was quite clear.

Several colleagues have also reminded me that even when one "leaves town," ties to hearts, stories, and generosity remain: Mary Grace Royal, you know what I mean, and Freda Gardner, a friend who will always be in my "balcony" of cherished wise-ones. Heartfelt thanksgiving and not a little shy wonder also go to Marguerite Shuster, who with a dry wit and tenacious spirit companioned me faithfully for *years* while I wrestled the angels; Sr. Shirley Nugent, who smiled her impish wisdom into my own unknown wounds and held me in hope as I began to heal; Paula Jeanne Teague, who showed me compassion does live and love beyond holy anger, which must be shared for intimacy to grow; and to Joyce Tucker, who opened doors even while she then had to endure the youthful impatience of those who entered. As holy havoc ensued and wrought what I now understand within this work, companions grounded in the covenantal promises of Spirit held my path true, especially Laurie Ferguson and Sharon Trekell. I hope you both see a small harvest here from the energies and prayers you shared, precisely when I needed them.

For all those in the Wabash family who challenge and nourish the best in the world of the academy, my gratitude does rise a bit like incense, though it is amongst the strawberries, good food, and stellar company, of course. Most especially, I offer thanks and heartfelt appreciation to Mary Elizabeth Mullino Moore whose work in the "field of the heart" never seems to get lost in the delights and demands of disciplinary precision and contribution. Your faithful advocacy, gentle wisdom, and unwielding courage—gifts you give to those whose lives you touch—will continue to form generations to come.

Beyond a doubt, none of this would have blossomed had I not stumbled into and been claimed by Spirit in the mysterious and mundane realities of radically covenantal companionship. Brian, my first love, I offer thanksgiving for the wonderful and confusing year so long ago. Anamcara, gratitude beyond words for your faithfulness, your integrity, your compassion, your delight, not to mention your last minute editing. And Brian, my life's love and God's blessed companion for me, your passion for the gospel, tenacity of trust, vulnerable devotion, and generous forgiveness have shaped more of this work than your Minnesotan reserve easily perceives. As we say, *Soli Deo Gloria* and blessed be.

Lisa M. Hess
Dayton, Ohio
November 28, 2008

Introduction

Paradox and surprise face those who pursue deeper spiritual practice, theological wisdom, even a religious calling "into the ministry." Many churches, denominations, and seminaries deepen the discipleship through which one relates to God or the sacred, as well as to traditions of people seeking a vibrant life of significance and service. They provide the resources and knowledge necessary for engaging the wisdom of countless generations. Unfortunately, these very same institutions can just as regularly fragment the gift of faith that had spurred the desire, the pursuit of wisdom, in the first place. The yearning for connection and faith, recognizable in expressive wonder and risked compassion, becomes stilted into a willed duty of institutional maintenance. Self-sacrificing professionalism somehow fosters an inability to receive ongoing spiritual nourishment. *Artisanal Theology* has been written to name and redress the divergence between the instigating relational formation of leaders in covenantal companionship and the necessarily programmatic education offered by institutionally- or traditionally-defined theological education.

I write in appreciation and support of those who likewise see a disparity. I write to invite even more conversation about the formation of religious leadership able to live and lead into hope amidst grief and change. And, not least, I offer some guidance for covenantal life within today's institutional ecology of congregation, academy, and denomination/tradition. The reasons for fragmentation and disconnection are legion, being dependent upon environmental, situational, and personal factors of all kinds. For my part, I have found great joy within the resources of theological institutions today—both congregations and academic institutions—yet my deepest hungers of faith and its grace-filled contributions have had to be nourished beyond the bounds of these communities. This is therefore a resource or handbook for those seeking to deepen their spiritual practice toward lived theological wisdom, either in companionship with a small group or in more formal theological study. It is not primarily for analysis or interpretation, but for sustenance on the quest for deeper practice and shared wisdom. Others in their way describe a journey for life abundant,[1] which both differs from and resonates with the intention here.

That said, the radically covenantal companionship undergirding this work can never be programmatically or institutionally created, which is both a good sign and a critical weakness for any theological book. In one sense, *Artisanal Theology* is more witness and less argument; more poetry to convert the spirit, less "how-to" technique to implement in communities. It remains a theological text because of the extensive resources received within the classical theological disciplines and years of clinical pastoral education which allowed this sense of radically covenantal companionship to be borne in experience, now birthed as book. It is intended for theological education and religious leadership formation today, even if its seeds, development, and fruits may not be immediately recognizable by many theologians I value as fellow educators and colleagues.

COMPANIONSHIPS:
COVENANTAL AND RADICALLY COVENANTAL

For clarity's sake, *companionship* names the public expression of human community and social civility today—the strength of weak ties[2] for broadest social cohesion. Etymologically, of course, it means those who break bread with one another. Practically, I see it in obviously purposed and well-structured human groups such as knitting circles, running clubs, book groups, tour travelers, classmates, perhaps even political rallies, and the like. *Covenantal* companionship can be seen in those partnerships and groups who share a common religious affiliation, who relatively easily identify the faith commitment and perspective of one another, or who advocate within tolerant alliances of shared understandings of faith, ideology, class, etc. Well-known and interpreted traditions speak of God's covenants with humanity, given shape in relation to Noah, to Abraham and Sarah, to Moses. Christians understand a life of the new covenant

1. Bass, *For Life Abundant.*
2. Granovetter, "The Strength of Weak Ties."

in the life, death, and resurrection of Jesus Christ. In each case, it is the organizing logic of a third presence or Presence that moves the companionship out of pragmatic social purposes and into much broader webs of relationship inspired by Word, sacrament, ritual, and mission. *Covenantal companionship*, as I intend it here, names the shared life of faith in today's contemporary religious communities, articulating or searching for the shared identity of tradition.

Radically covenantal companionship, however, grows from within both unidentified and covenantal companionships to press the life-giving force and integrity of sacred-human relationship beyond the normative boundaries of social or even religious affiliation. In contrast to public or traditionally-oriented companionships, radical covenant embodies an intimate interdependence of all sentient beings in the lively web of creation. While previously inconceivable to me, its origins in my own life are fairly mundane. I first had an inkling of it in a formally structured group process stewarded by professionals trained in interpersonal and group development. It grew into a less structured but quite intentional form through coaching and spiritual direction. Among other gifts, coaching brings persistent attention to the goodness intended, made possible within a collaboratively examined, wisely experimental life. Spiritual direction facilitates awakening and hones communal listening for God's presence toward holy intent as grace gradually unfolds in the mysterious and the mundane. My sense of covenant grew broader and deeper into maturity within marriage, in which (alongside my husband) I learn the vulnerable and renewing love that forms and transforms each of us to live more fully into the world. Most recently, the sense of radical covenant blossomed anew in a spiritual or holy friendship, which I now know has centuries of historical precedent within Christian, Jewish, Islamic/Sufi, and Buddhist traditions (and probably more).[3] Each and all of these socially identifiable relationships have nuanced the articulation given here of what I'm calling radically covenantal companionship. It is witnessed within all wisdom traditions. It is becoming more frequently observable within seeking populations today. Its unpredictable yet trustworthy life undergirds a discipleship that enlivens and challenges, wounds and heals, discomforts and nourishes. But it is only to be received, not willed or

3. See Aelred of Rievaulx, *Spiritual Friendship*; Addison and Breitman, *Jewish Spiritual Direction*; Rumi, *The Glance*; Subhuti, *Buddhism and Friendship*; and Weaver and Messer, *Connected Spirits*.

instigated by practice and technique. Even worse, it cannot be taught, though in today's globalized worlds I dare say it *must* be learned.

DAILY BREAD

I therefore have no pretensions that this little volume will produce radically covenantal companionship, even with my own evangelical fervor about it. Relational formation is primarily messy, unpredictable, highly subjective, and nearly impossible to evaluate. More and more theological education environments struggle to create residential communities in which covenantal companionships may be fostered. All of us face real dangers in this quest too. Attempting relationally-formative practices in today's legalistic and highly polarized cultures promises intractable challenges of unhealthy relationships, potential power-abuse, and more. Spiritual intimacy is *not* for the faint of heart.[4] It absolutely assumes adult learners, able to assess and discern both benefits and risks in spiritual formation. Yet the gifts of God for peace, unity, and purity—rooted deep within historical traditions and steeped in primarily relational assumptions—seem less and less probable without some redress. Awareness of "community" that superficially mimics the biblical and theological covenantal community needs to grow. The organic life of theological wisdom, renewed in a disciplined spiritual stewardship of self, lived world, and the uncontrollable Holy, must be retrieved from seductive dissections.

One starting place within my own reach is the ministry of formation-integration at a regional Christian seminary. *Artisanal Theology* is a resource for this daily bread, the continued learning of God's purposes amongst theological students and faculty with whom I serve. Here I hope to introduce theological seekers and students to a primarily relational but theologically-integrated way of thinking begun in covenantal groups. In many institutions of theological learning, these groups offer the best vehicle for re-learning community, engaging pastoral practice, and experimenting with diversity of all kinds. They are the stopgap between all the disciplinary departments, the glue that somehow continues to hold together increasingly specialized education and widely diverse lives of ministry. Faculty, formed within doctoral studies today, have no reason or reward to pursue their disciplines in such primarily relational fashion. No wonder many theological faculties—impossibly stretched and

4. Schnarch, *Passionate Marriage*, 100.

disciplinarily divided as we are today—offer few resources with which to value, observe, or participate easily in what I write here. I do not believe that will ever change, nor am I convinced it *should* change. But theological faculties yearn just as much as anyone for a life of contribution, significance, shared wisdom, even expressive delight. There *is* sustenance here for the spiritually hungry, whether one is a seeker, potential theological student, or professional theologian.

The path cannot and will not remain within the struggling environments of theological institutions, however. All kinds of small groups—be they in mega-church congregations or virtual and emergent communities—yearn for a spiritually formative method and end-goal whereby they may deepen their practice and live theological wisdom into the world's greatest hungers. Guidance is direly needed for creating covenantal communities and then identifying and fostering the radically covenantal companionships potentially within them. Theological resources abound with which to live into deeper practice, theological wisdom, but only when the life of expressive delight beckons, able to companion the suffering of self and others. Orthodoxy and heresy were for another time long gone. As I harp on it with my own students and anyone else who will listen alongside me, I think today's fundamental questions center in the inevitable of any era: how to love who and what one fears, in chosen compassion, integrity, and wisdom. An artisanal theology aims to invite conversation and theological integration toward wisdom within and beyond theological learning environments. An expressive and companionable delight then awaits us all.

STRUCTURE OF THE BOOK

Chapter 1 delves more deeply into the felt-dissonances between today's rhetorical "communities" of "covenant" and the vibrant realities of community and covenant through which an intentional formation promises an artisanal theology for faith known in delight. Formation, theological education, wisdom, and ministry are defined before encompassing objectives for formation within theological education today are offered. Artisanal theology may then take shape as the traditionally inherited and embodied theology recognizable in delight and rooted in radically covenantal companionship. Some final preliminaries, specifically for those inquiring into formal theological study, conclude the chapter.

God's covenantal community and the expansive world of spiritual stewardship within which covenant becomes palpable finds expression in chapter 2. Relying on the conceptual work of Dorothy Holland and her colleagues,[5] three "worlds" within theological education—the local congregation, tradition or denominational heritage, and the academy—chart the terrain whereby personal identity and covenant form in mutual and dynamic relationship. The witness in tradition and contemporary voices for a wisdom way of knowing—what is named here as an unpredictable knowing toward wisdom—gives some guidance into the counter-intuitive wisdom of relational knowing. The disciplined spiritual stewardship necessary to sustain and participate in such unpredictability is then introduced before moving into the processes of spiritual autobiography and contextual reflection that structure a more relationally centered knowledge.

Chapter 3 describes this storied way of knowing through which an intentional formation begins to shape human selves and covenantal companionships toward a shared and shaping wisdom. Personal stories shared within covenantal companionships lead to self-discovery, communal belonging, and unexpected transformation. The common resistances to this way of knowing and to sharing one's stories are reviewed before moving to constructive tasks to be considered within companionship. Critical practices of spiritual autobiography and contextual analysis enflesh this way of knowing by demonstrating the *how* of personal stories, shared and critically engaged in increasingly broader contexts toward a mutually discerned sense of God's Story come to life in particular events and experiences. The chapter concludes with guidelines for covenantal relationship that lives God's unconditional promise into these contexts.

Chapter 4 brings this storying and being storied within communities of covenant into the broader context of theological traditions that have been formed to give entrances into God's Story within a variety of resources. This is merely preparatory for an articulate telling of the Story of God in today's professional and religious climate. Classical and pragmatic lenses portray theology in many of its rooms. The practical theological perspective offered here resembles Edward Farley's "interpretation of situations,"[6] but broadens it beyond an easily assumed, textual interpre-

---

5. Holland, Lachicotte, Skinner, and Cain, *Identity and Agency in Cultural Worlds*, 49ff.

6. Farley, *Practicing Gospel*, 29–43.

tation. An artisanal theology lives particular energies—delight, wonder, passion, celebration, as well as holy anger, lament, and frustration—into reflective practices shared in communities, both intimate and difficult. This integrative work, aimed toward an artisanal theology, requires both intimately disclosive experiences of God's present actions and mutually discerned paths into established and peripheral traditions of faith. The goal is to encourage and guide discoveries of personal voice and contribution amidst the overwhelming number of perspectives available.

Chapter 5 offers my own artisanal loaf, a unique rendition of an articulate theology crafted within an intentional formation and disciplined spiritual stewardship. The statement offers my experience and understanding of who God is and how the Story lives within a particular but communal (North American) setting today. One purpose is to demonstrate a historically situated "end-product" of the formal process articulated in previous chapters. Any contextual theology must necessarily witness to particularity and personal story as they become somehow revelatory of the grace and refining mercy of the living God. The notes accompanying the text acknowledge resources, but also are intended to instruct and interpret the process itself. An epilogue offers some final observations about theological delight and radically covenantal companionships. Appendices for facilitating group processes are included as well. In the end, *Artisanal Theology* is only a recipe for whatever readers will make of it.

1

Intentional Formation toward an Artisanal Theology

Too many of us who form religious leadership today have had our own lives and desire for God distracted from that covenantal delight that is one of the strongest antidotes to the cynicism and apathy facing many religious communities. Consider "Linda," age sixty-two. She is a successful Protestant pastor, well esteemed by her congregation. She was a select contributor to a clergy-congregational renewal initiative. When given space and anonymity to speak plainly, she spoke a weary truth: "I was most cut-off from God when I was at my most excellent." She spoke of the seventy to eighty-hour work weeks, on-call pastoral visits, interrupted holidays with family, unending communal and cultural demands of "church" as conceived today. Her yearning for a life-affirming, balanced way to enjoy God within her own spirit *and* serve God in a community was palpable . . . and repeatedly distracted. She knew her congregation had little awareness of just how arid her own experience of the Holy had become over the years.

"Charles," non-ordained and forty-six years old, faced a similar challenge between healthy nourishment of his relationship with God in his local congregation and the overwhelming demands of congregational leadership. He grew up culturally Christian and devoted sizable time and energies to the educational life of his faith community, particularly youth. He "did church" well, though always felt something was missing. Imagine his surprise when he awoke to a Presence unforeseen but immediately recognizable and joyfully received. Humility, deep joy, and intimate spiritual companionship now inform his spiritual path, suspected but previously unknown, unimagined by him or his family but clearly attested in Christian scriptures, unpredictable but known by the Spirit's fruits of faith, delight, and compassion. He said, "How did I not know, for so long, that there was so much more to be received? Now *this* is religion!" He

1

remains a member of his local congregation, but must participate at some distance. The vibrant experience of the Holy and his intentional journey of faith have become nearly incomprehensible to most others in his worship community.

I have had to confront this tension myself. I grew up in a local Christian congregation that I still treasure. They gave me structure when I needed it, as well as when I did not want it. They gave me space to pursue a faith journey at some distance, and then welcomed me home again. My young adult years were rich with educational resources in the sciences, as well as in formal theological education. I have lived in urban cosmopolitan settings, smaller towns, and suburban communities, all of which have sheltered and stretched my curious spirit. I received grace upon grace within established institutions of theological learning and have been companioned by wise elders of faith—within my own family as well as with those met along the way. Imagine my surprise, then, when I began to learn of the radically covenantal companionship that fed my being and fired my spirit. It was the life of the words I had heard all my life, but beyond anything I had ever known, anything I had ever learned in previous congregational and educational settings. Institutions of theological life and learning seemed a logical place to pursue wisdom, but I discovered that for numerous reasons they harbored few resources for primarily relational formation of spirit-mind-body. What to do? Join the tradition of resource manuals,[1] apparently, and write what I see. Do you see it too?

CONTEMPORARY CHALLENGES IN CONTEXTS

There are two threads within contemporary contexts that shape what is to come here: community and the potential captivity of knowledge when "community" refers only to those who think like us or believe what we do.

"Community" does not mean what has been historically assumed or even theologically described in classical resources. Spiritually seeking people enter into religious communities in order to eat what they have been told is a feast. In fact, what they often receive, with little attention to their own self-history and awareness, is precisely the opposite. Communally prescribed duties of "church" and irresponsible self-sacrifice are common

1. For example, Macek, "Advice Manuals and the Formation of English Protestant and Catholic Clerical Identities."

fare of many religious institutions today. Faithful members of well-meaning congregations spend inordinate time attempting to reconcile their felt loneliness while living a "religious" life that is overly busy with work for congregation and tradition. Religious leaders gain the training and certification required for professional competence, yet become disconnected from what or Who drew them into a religious vocation at the very beginning. It all looks like "community," but there is little deepening intimacy or relationship that assuages the hidden loneliness. Few religious leaders I know are able, amidst the overwhelming demands of congregational ministry today, to relish their own family lives or foster a delight that empowers companionship of the stranger, the lost, the poor. Community has become "social enclave," with little awareness about the yearnings of "the other."

A related thread, therefore, is what it means to know and act, theologically, in such "communities." With little authentic, intimate relationship, knowledge becomes information and interpretation, unhinged from personal contexts or communal understandings and identity. For instance, it has become commonplace to disrespect not only disagreement but the personhood of those with whom we disagree. No longer are all sources of information to be heard, but only the ones within those "communities" recognizable or in closest alliance to us. Self-awareness and awakening to a larger public, a larger world in which all may thrive, become overwhelming and too threatening within so many disagreements and diverse voices. Persons become disconnected from themselves, learning to distrust their own senses. In fear of being overwhelmed, they hold onto familiar ignorance in the face of information from "communities" not their own. Theological wisdom communities, on the other hand, challenge such "communal" practices of knowledge that focus inwardly and without appreciation for the other.

What do I mean by the theologically wise? They are those for whom humility received in a life-sustaining covenant fosters endurance, character, hope, and love, even in the face of whatever worldly logics enthrall us all today. Rooted covenant such as this empowers interest in detachment, strength in weakness, delight in service. There is great passion felt by the self for the world and all its peoples yet the self increasingly disappears from notice. In a situation of great pain or trauma, wisdom urges an unknowing without answers, a sacrifice of any "professional expertise" or role. Instead, the wise enact a communal strength in quiet companionship. A *theo*-logical professional[2] may assert an authority in the face of mercilessly exercised power, but it is a vulnerable assertion, done from a wealth of joy in the offering. Only in the roots of covenantal companionship can self-sacrifice on behalf of the grieving, the powerless, and the silenced be chosen in such vulnerable joy. Such acts rest upon a covenantal logic through which situations can be subverted. Injustice, violence, and radical suffering are confronted with love, in the name of hope, however faint. "Community" in name becomes transformed into an interdependent community. Knowledge becomes intimate acquaintance in service of advocacy. I know nothing in this world able to promise such unworldly ends, *except* the covenantal companionship that flows through others and back to the One who calls each of us beyond ourselves, into the world.

Our best hope for theological wisdom must therefore be a communal and covenantal one of intentional formation. In order to receive the wisdom of those who have come before us, each of us needs other people—their stories, their experience, even their touch. Today's confusion surrounding "community" creates a need for much greater guidance about the kind of community that sustains and nourishes. We need to remember, or learn anew, the covenantal community with its particularly subversive and life-giving charisms witnessed in most religious traditions. More and more of us, particularly within North American contexts of self-sufficiency and individualism, fail to receive any explicit direction in what this kind of covenantal community actually entails, in both challenges and graces. Until this conundrum of deeper spiritual practice and theological wisdom is explored and constructively redressed through intentional formation in covenantal companionship, those seeking spiritual nourishment will continue to be seduced into lives of faith that bind themselves and others. Those whose desire propels them into formal programs of theological education and certification will continue to become religious leaders whose public lives of service disconnect themselves and others from discipleship in a faith of expressive and companionable delight.

2. This italics' emphasis refers to the paradoxical challenge of speaking or living God into a finite world, named especially well in Jean-Luc Marion's work, *God Without Being*, 139ff.

USE OF TERMS? INTENTIONAL FORMATION, THEOLOGICAL EDUCATION, WISDOM, AND MINISTRY

All this begs the questions of what *intentional formation* is, by definition,[3] and how that phenomenon relates to theological education, wisdom, and ministry. Formation here simply refers to that *shaping-and-being-shaped* experienced by real people living their lives within intimate and broader socio-cultural environments. The temptation within established institutions, led by faithful and competent professionals, is to focus energies on *what* formation is for the religious identity of future leaders. Know that, aim for that, then formation will result. Yet knowing *about* something has its own limitations. Knowing about ice-skating, for instance, does not insure any ability to skate on the ice. Similarly, knowing *what* formation is does not insure any intentional participation in it whatsoever. Dissatisfaction about formation in theological education—the only real consensus among scholars and practitioners[4]—arises from focusing on the *what*, from overwhelmingly too much knowledge, too many perspectives, and little confirmed awareness of the gifts and wisdom already present. Plenty of knowledge already exists to order faithful action, to celebrate *what is*, with limitation right alongside potential. More often than not, however, formation in theological education refers to a specialized discipline with a practical focus. It names the contextual and integrative work of leadership identity and development, understood as the responsibility or expertise of those practically trained, not that of the theological learning community as a whole.

Which brings us to theological education. Whenever I refer to *theological education*, I mostly mean the formal institutional processes marked by graduate degree programs in "divinity." It is how the two-word term usually functions in most of the environments I know. All of us in this enterprise, however, know that any theological wisdom gained through theological education today involves local communities, wise mentors, unexpected or even significance-threatening life events, internal desire, struggle, and a rhythm of departure and return to covenant

3. Foster, Dahill, Goleman, and Tolentino, *Educating Clergy*, offers an excellent summary of contemporary understandings of formation within formal theological education. Examined in Lisa M. Hess, "Formation in the Worlds of Theological Education," 14–23. Two other formative resources have been Carroll, Wheeler, Aleshire, and Marler, *Being There*, and Klimoski, "The Evolving Dynamics of Formation."

4. Foster et al., *Educating Clergy*, 125–26 n.1.

within faith communities. Even more broadly, faith education for all happens every Sunday—or Saturday or Friday, depending upon one's faith
community—amidst practices of worship, scriptural study, communal
fellowship, and service of others. Worldviews are solidified or challenged
in *this* kind of education every week. But theological education, as I will
use it, refers pragmatically to formal degree programs that continue to
focus the imagination and contributions of religious and theological faculty, seminary administrators, and students entering into such programs
across the United States.

I place a lot of emphasis on theological *wisdom* here, which lives
between the cracks of a formal theological education and any practice of
ministry or the life of discipleship. Contemplative Cynthia Bourgeault has
recently shaped a sense of this term,[5] which stands alongside the exist-
ing discourse about it in the discipline of practical theology.[6] Bourgeault
acknowledges both popular and formal nuances of the term "wisdom"—
popular practical guidance, wisdom literature, gift of contemplation—but
defines it for her own work as "a precise and comprehensive science of
spiritual transformation that has existed since the headwaters of the great
world religions and is in fact their common ground."[7] She describes wisdom as "a way of knowing that goes beyond one's mind, one's rational
understanding, and embraces the whole of a person."[8] She reaches into
ancient and admittedly esoteric strands of Christian, Jewish, and Sufi traditions to stretch highly cognitive and technological ways of knowing to
include what actually becomes newly visible and understandable within a
life of spiritual discipline, communal service, and receptive grace. She describes a way of living into wisdom in human experience with a rhythm
of freedom and surrender, which becomes important for the description
of covenantal companionship here.

In contrast to her definition, intentional formation in covenantal
companionship cannot rightly be called a *science* of transformation, at
least without leading to misunderstanding in an obsessively scientific and
reactionarily religious society. But such intentional formation *is* a similar template or lived pattern in which wisdom-knowing is transmitted,
traditioned, cherished, from one generation to another. Indefinable yet

5. Bourgeault, *The Wisdom Way of Knowing: Reclaiming an Ancient Tradition to Awaken the Heart*.

6. See Browning, *A Fundamental Practical Theology*, and Warford, *Practical Wisdom*.

7. Bourgeault, *Wisdom Way of Knowing*, xvi–xvii.

8. Ibid., 27–28.

intimately recognizable, wisdom in these pages refers to that living, primarily relational and embodied—Real—source of insight, significance, meaning, and purpose. Intentional formation within established institutions of theological education is an integrative, wisdom path through which covenantal community returns companions to themselves with delight and into the world in service. It is a wisdom way of knowing in which companionship invites, shapes, and sends persons into the world to give freely, receive unexpectedly, and live within a service that is chosen but not willed.

Ministry describes this service, though it also has some contemporary imbalances that need redress. In its deepest sense, the term refers to those risked acts of compassion and sharing where persons, so moved and intimately involved, open to an uncertain encounter with the Sacred, who returns them to the community empowered to serve. I have known ministry to be received and empowered in the person of Jesus Christ, in the power of the Spirit. I also know that this ministry has been observed with those who would not use that language at all, whether they have been Buddhists, Jews, agnostics, or others. In ministry, persons are ministered to, each by the other, Each within the Other. In my own Presbyterian faith, every member of the church is understood to be a minister of the congregation, which suggests a broad understanding of the word. This would surprise many of these same members, because "ministry" within many Protestant settings in North America carries with it disconcerting imbalances: ministry to the poor by the wealthy, ministry to the people by the clergy, ministry to *them* from *us*.[9] Rare is the understanding of the actual implications of ministry, at its broadest: human interdependence and shared human identity across categories. Without this understanding, ministry becomes a detached activity for others, provided by human selves. The imbalance stymies congregations from living into what classical theological traditions call *koinonia*, or the *"fellowship-creating reality* of Christ's presence in the world."[10] Without *koinonia*, ministry is a profession and an employment. In sum and without fault or blame, ministry today usually refers to those who have or are pursuing formal theological education, who are going into the ministry as a professional pursuit and gainful employment.

9. Bell, "The Teachers," *He Was In the World*, 15–17. Ministry in his sense is "the necessary interaction between those who seem to be deprived or disabled and those who think that they are alright."

10. Lehmann, *Ethics in a Christian Context*, 49.

OBJECTIVES OF FORMATION

Intentional formation may be further clarified with reference to its objectives within theological education. Formation in disciplinary discourse identifies a relatively young, interdisciplinary area of scholarship and relational integration in which the various theological disciplines are brought to bear on discipleship lived in the multiple publics all of us face today. As an area of relational integration, it is guided by counter-intuitive wisdom and requires capacities and practices that bridge texts and people within relationally centered contexts. Intentional formation describes a less disciplinarily oriented and more holistic path toward Bourgeault's wisdom way of knowing, integrative of formal theological education but not constrained by its specialization.

These objectives have been refined within contexts of analytical-conceptual clarity, skeptical-cynical debates, and impassioned-idealistic envisioning with many others. They can be summarized easily in a bullet-list fashion, but they are not to be achieved as much as to stimulate a life of learning and pursuit of wisdom within communities of spiritual practice. Lists also (unfortunately) suggest an order of importance, so perhaps the objectives can be placed in a mental circle, or better yet, a sphere. Imagine a sphere in which each objective intermingles with all the others, making a complete whole. Intentional formation aims for

a. a rooted self-confidence rooted *not* in the self

b. self-awareness through differentiation toward self-acceptance, witnessed in an expressive delight

c. healthily bounded relationships with others, those served and serving

d. a practiced willingness to sustain healthy conflict and navigate ambiguity with love

e. a particular faith identity (Christian, Jewish, Muslim, Hindi, Buddhist, etc.) heightened by a deep, participatory listening, willingness to be shaped by others

f. an ability to articulate learning and to discover new questions

g. a supple theological vision founded in hope and lived within Spirit

Notice how the textual requirements of subject areas within formal theological education—fourfold theological disciplines of Bible, history, theology, and practice—are left implicit. Textual articulation of tradition is not *un*important, but it is also not the ultimate aim. A life in God lived into concrete and embodied forms and observable in devotion, compassion, delight, playful service, joy, celebration, wonder—these are the relational points that can be deepened and given concrete historical witness within the critical and textual resources of the disciplines. These relational mysteries of faith only become more remarkable, more real, more historically palpable when pursued and confirmed within theological traditions. Nonetheless, the textual traditions must not obscure God's invitation to deeper intimacy and covenantal discipleship, unto union with God, who gives significance, meaning, and purpose.

Intentional formation requires a well-examined commitment to a living tradition, lived in an embodied spirit and by means of devotion (objective *e*). Living traditions[11] require participatory listening and a willingness to be shaped by the argument lived by others in particular covenantal communities. A particular faith-identity professes this primary commitment to others' lives through a fierce but humble devotion to the One (with many names) who creates and reconciles us all. Paradoxically, that commitment cannot be made or sustained unless there is a confident (or at least assured) self, rooted not in the self and therefore made continually more aware (objective *a*). Any life lived intentionally in human relationships will demonstrate egos large and small, those hungry for public affirmation of all kinds and those who have long since sacrificed their sense of self without ever knowing their own value. Selves rooted in themselves run in oft-destructive suffering, their own and that of others. In contrast, selves known and claimed, yet mysteriously unimportant or absent, manifest a creative agency and compassion seen only in the fruits received over time. Lived wisdom, in other words. These selves somehow appear rooted, yet not rigid; assured and vibrant, yet strangely supple and flexible. There is a self-acceptance alongside a continual thirst for deeper roots yet unseen.

Within living wisdom traditions, intentional formation fosters this rooted-not-rooted self-confidence or self-acceptance in a particular and complex process available only within communities of covenant, whether

11. See MacIntyre, *After Virtue*, 222.

implicit or explicit at this point. Self-acceptance that sustains human persons only comes through greater and greater self-awareness, or repeated discoveries of shadow[12] and light, strength, and frailty (part 1 of objective *b*). Differentiation from other selves, while maintaining relationship and interdependence,[13] is the culturally counter-intuitive path to this self-awareness and acceptance (part 2, objective *b*). It requires a practiced willingness to sustain conflict and ambiguity for a deeper theological interconnectedness (objective *d*). Interconnectedness that witnesses to a truly theological intimacy means being known, frailties and all, and *loved anyway* with unmerited, unachieved grace. Intimacy like this does not diffuse individuality, but heightens it in a constitutive relationality uncontrolled by either self-in-relation.[14] Humans cannot love like this, independently, but God does love like this through self-differentiated and unexpectedly compassionate human beings.

Healthily-bounded, covenantal relationships with others (objective *c*) create the holding-space for greater self-awareness toward self-acceptance. Surprisingly, truly covenantal communities will accept us more readily than we can accept ourselves. Those who live God's unconditional yet demanding acceptance into their shared lives introduce best *how* to accept all of who we are, shadow and all. The result is an expressive delight that cannot be contained, but overflows with an unending compassion, commitment, and love for one and all (part 3, objective *b*). *Un*healthy relationships, those *not* sustained within a covenant for the good of the other, often keep us in "hamster wheel suffering,"[15] or a forced and painful acceptance of an imprisoned and imprisoning self, not able to participate fully, more deeply, in truly intimate relationships. I have learned to look for the delight, the passion, or the spark of outward interest to get a sense of another's self-awareness, level of differentiation, and wizened acceptance of the human condition lived in divine grace.

Intentional formation, glimpsed in these objectives, fosters an ability to articulate learning and discover new questions (objective *f*). Sustained over time, grace-filled insights and the artistry of a living wisdom tradition begin to form a supple theological vision, founded in hope and lived

---

12. See Johnson, *Owning Your Own Shadow*.

13. Schnarch, *Passionate Marriage*, 56.

14. Loder, *Logic of the Spirit*, 254.

15. Engelmann, *Running in Circles*, 26ff.

within the Spirit of God (objective *g*). A vision is not only a grandiose or idealistic improbability, as today's fear-ridden and empirical pundits would have us believe. Visions are little phrases, gifted in flashes of insight and lived into unexpected vibrancy over time within covenantal community. "Begin with what you know, but do not remain there." "Open." "It is about delight." "Inconvenient, isn't it?" Those are some of my own phrases, and they have led to what I share here. The objectives are intended only to guide and suggest a deeper theological knowledge toward lived wisdom, available with the most rooted theological traditions and assured selves we can practice.

ARTISANAL THEOLOGY?

Intentional formation refers, in the end, to the *how* of an integrated theological wisdom. Many today will disdain the mundane *how* of such a process, often relegated to the unimportant or uninteresting. As Fred Craddock observes, "Perhaps no word among us has suffered more abuse than *how*. Not the honorable abuse of attack, but the humiliating abuse of inattention, disregard, slight. *How* has been made to stand out in the hall while *what* was being entertained by the brightest minds among us." [16] We need to return again to a more practical question: *How* may those drawn into pursuits of wisdom participate in deepening spiritual practices with a grace and fidelity to who (and whose) they are, and with satisfaction and imagination for long-lived life in God, for the other, in the world? We need guidance for harvesting the resources already available within our living traditions. We need a way to honor the complexity and duration of the pursuit of theological wisdom. Spiritual practices require time and surrender, actions of spirit able to counteract an ingrained, cultural impatience of all participants. We need a rigorous yet perhaps more poetic approach to theology, ministry, and the unruly but delightful demands of both. Borrowing from long-standing bakers' wisdom, I suggest the term *artisanal* for consideration and adaptation.

Baking bread as a Sabbath practice over years of service in theological institutions has led me to deepening spiritual practice and a new sense of theological wisdom, both of which regularly shape my continued formation in theology and ministry. In bread-baking, *artisanal* refers to classical, traditionally-rooted, yet reasonably modernized ways to bake

16. Craddock, *Overhearing the Gospel*, 4–5.

bread from scratch in one's own kitchen, or even a small bakery. Loaves are uniquely crafted by hand and some modern conveniences, but only those chosen to sustain the most favorable integration of flavor, function, and artistry. *Artisanal* names those who refuse to release their primary focus upon the interpersonal and untidy transmission of wisdom, even in the seductive challenges and gifts of (post-)modernity[17] and mass-production. The result is reasonably efficient but uniquely crafted loaves of bread, delightful not only in nutritious sustenance but also in personalized characters of texture, crumb, crust, and appearance. If you want a loaf of bread immediately, the grocery provides store-bought bread that is both less costly and quicker. Such bread rarely draws a community together for the purposes of flavor and fellowship, however. Such bread does not communicate the human touch so necessary for sustained companionship, which can then share delight in a feast and can strengthen others in adversity.

This kind of bread-baking has slowly evolved for me over the years into what some would call a *Sabbath practice*, a weekly discipline or activity in which ceasing, resting, embracing, and feasting form and re-form a God-centered rhythm in body, mind, and spirit.[18] I inherited a classical yet modernized kitchen-wisdom from my father and an appreciation of the shared delights from my mother. I gained courage to hear my own practice of bread-baking as a means of wisdom and grace from Brother Peter Reinhart, a lay-member of Christ the Savior Brotherhood and a culinary instructor who has drawn repeated connections between bread-baking and a path of spiritual formation.[19] The practice itself is fairly mundane. Once weekly, I mix select ingredients and knead them by machine, and then by hand into their proper feel and form. I am returned to my senses, mindful of the aromas of the yeast and the push and pull of the forming gluten strands of the dough. Sometimes I find myself thinking of my father and his own inherited style. Other times I experiment with new shapes and pressure. Next, I have to wait an uncertain time in order for the dough to rise. Repeatedly, I have to learn how difficult and how necessary it is to slow down for the natural fermentation process to do its work in the dough. When it is finally time, I punch the dough down to

---

17. See Ploeger, *Dare We Observe?*
18. See Dawn, *Keeping the Sabbath Wholly*. See also her *The Sense of the Call*.
19. See Reinhart, *Bread Upon the Waters*.

release some of the yeast's efforts and knead it for a second rising. I have to wait again. I may have to wait for a third time for the dough to rise within the loaf pans or clay dish of a *La Cloche* hearth-oven. Whenever the loaves are ready, I bake them for an hour or less in a conventional oven. Taking the loaves from the oven, I used to think the practice was complete. True to Sabbath intentions, I have since learned that the final step is a mindful, fully embodied, communal enjoyment of the loaf.

Thinking back on it, my mother did teach me the delight of the crusty heel, sopped with butter. Her eyes would light up as Dad brought it to her, either on a plate or simply a paper towel. His eyes would light up too, as such things can be contagious. More recently, my own local community taught me the delight of sharing loaves of my bread, resulting in a bread label, of sorts: *The Sabbatical Bakery*, "because everyone needs a little extra dough." Reinhart makes many more connections, but his essay on "What is an Artisanal Loaf?" solidified the distinction of artisanal for this Sabbath practice of bread-baking.[20]

Artisanal, then, names the primarily relational transmission of craft and wisdom to be shared within and beyond one's communities of knowledge. Participants rely upon the resources and conveniences available in order to offer not only a variability of artistic products, but also a shared delight in that variability, that unique formation. A Sabbath intention gives theological characteristics to the artisanal notion—surrender to shaping, humility of participation (not control) in a creative process, feasting on and sharing of creative expressions. In my bread-baking, for example, I shape the loaves, but am also shaped myself by a creative rhythm and complex fermentation over which I have little control. I am the baker, but only one agent in a very lively creative process. The normal routines of my week cease, and there is opportunity to rest, celebrate, and even feast upon creation (and creativity's bounty) with a delight that embraces others. This multi-layered metaphor originates with Reinhart's work, particularly the concept of humility met with grace. Unexpected things often happen with a batch of dough, and yet these unexpected bumps, with surrender and grace, become an added texture or flavor.

To describe a theological method and perspective, *artisanal* holds together classical practices given voice in wise-elders and contemporary resources of all kinds to form a traditionally-rooted yet unknowing path

20. Reinhart, *Brother Juniper's Bread Book*, 157–63.

of theological wisdom. Like artisanal bread-bakers across the world, artisanal theologians honor the traditions living into new forms within and beyond them, even as they refuse to accommodate a technological rationality or modern project that prefers products to persons. In sum, an intentional formation suited to spiritual renewal and a pursuit of theological wisdom aims for a theory and practice of faith more like the artisanal loaf shaped within radical covenant, not a ready-made and pro-grammatic loaf shaped within theological education. *Artisanal theology* describes an articulate and traditionally-rooted faith perspective that is resourced, kneaded, stretched, even punched down and risen again within covenantal companionships sustained in contexts of church, denomination or tradition, and schools. A path through deeper spiritual practice toward theological wisdom engages intentional formation when listening for knowledge in a primarily communal way, through stories shared and the articulation of a contextual theology. An artisanal theology intentionally engages the historical and (post-)modern gifts of method and awareness within radically relational covenant lived in companionable delight on behalf of all.

DELIGHT

This kind of theological delight is not a willed happiness in the face of pain, nor is it a Pollyanna preference for the beautiful or cheerful aspects of living. True delight is intimately related to a capacity for wonder, not self-deception; risked trust, not assured clarity. Delight balances an attentive discipline of wonder with accurate seeing that may discomfort. Scientist-philosopher Michael Polanyi identifies this kind of delight in the intuited, then verifiable discovery of a scientific theory, for example.[21] This kind of delight also empowers a willing participation in suffering—one's own and that of others—with a strength and gratitude for what life already is, as life. Not the companionship of suffering fueled by a rage—no matter how righteous—or a wound received and left untended. Not the willed sacrifice of time and personhood based in "shoulds" and "oughts" taught by culture. A theological delight originates from compassion unexpectedly received, hidden wounds healed, undeserved love erupting into situations of injustice or poverty. This kind of delight is a gift from God, a grace that cannot be grasped or produced, imposed or taught.

21. Polanyi, *Personal Knowledge*, 133.

It can be received, however, through a quiet discipline and receptive practices in covenantal relationship. It is received through facing the pain of one's fears, wounds, limitations. It arrives unexpectedly after accepting the prickly realities of contemporary faith life. It comes amidst the hard work of prayer, in Roberta Bondi's sense: not discarding damaged parts of ourselves, but gathering and reclaiming them for daily healing in the presence of God.[22] Unexpectedly, undeservedly, in proportion to one's self-knowledge of true smallness, delight arrives, overflowing with an irrepressible joy. This is an observable paradox and felt-sensation of divinely intimate nobody-ness. It is received in the touch of a hand, or the brush of a breeze in a meadow. Amidst bustling populations of passers-by on a street corner in Kentucky,[23] or in a field full of sunflowers. With the aroma of freshly baked bread or the sacred heaviness of incense offered in glorious praise and prayer. Delight arrives, and then it cannot be contained. Even the most arid theological prose can witness to it and create within the believer's heart the seed that then blossoms in due season.

Artisanal theology as encouraged within this book is recognizable, regardless of tradition, by an expressive delight. Receptivity is key. Nothing quite matures an individual self for receptivity in faith like a community, though not in just any gathering. Healthy receptivity that sustains true intimacy must be one of covenant, rooted in the promises and merciful justice of the Holy, not in the needs or desires of other human beings. Covenantal community upholds the best self of each of us and mirrors failings in a gentle invitation to grow. It interprets and goads each of us into deeper and deeper expression of an articulate, interpersonally and traditionally-rooted life of faith and service. It meets our deepest hungers with God's most gracious nurture. Intentional formation toward an artisanal theology ultimately shapes a discipleship able to companion suffering from a received wealth of felt delight, able to participate in unexpected encounters of compassion.

YES, WRITING

The pursuit of deeper spiritual practice and theological wisdom within established institutions of theological education traditionally requires

---

22. Bondi, *Memories of God*, 33–35.

23. Merton, "Conjectures of a Guilty Bystander," in *Thomas Merton: Spiritual Master*, 144.

personal and communal practices of writing. Are these absolutely necessary for a life lived in a companionable delight? No, of course not. But writing helps self-awareness like little else I know. It's right up there with meditation and contemplative prayer, in my book. The act of writing invites you to commit to your own story and thought, made visible for all to see within your prose. You become aware, differentiate and align your story with that of a broader community of belonging, discourse, conviction. Particularly for those who have come to this path without a churched background, writing stories—and even theologies—offers a unique opportunity to explore personal identity within communal traditions, whether established or more peripheral.

An overt commitment to spiritual growth in writing communicates several things, to the self as well as to others. First, it reminds each of us of the limitations of perspectives and the need to practice a gentle patience alongside convictions. Many find themselves looking for authoritative voices that seem to promise an assurance or a confidence for what they want to say. This is natural, but it will not lessen the reality that perspectives are limited and narrow. Humility, gentle patience, and finitude are gifts to be received, if contrary to some professional norms of ministry. Writing also reveals unexpected thoughts, with greater clarity and ability to compare/contrast them with others. Self-awareness and accurate self-knowledge then grow, with attention and effort. Knowledge of God at the intersection of texts and contexts grows, breathed into human companions. Wisdom may even blossom, Lord willing. Writing ultimately pushes the author into a larger community of belonging and identity, made real in time. Committing thoughts to paper and public scrutiny allows others to find, support, and challenge the future becoming that God intends.

Regardless whether you like it or not, you have also received a faith perspective from your family, your own propensity to be curious, your favorite hymns, lived experiences of compassion or betrayal. Why write it instead of just knowing it, or talking about it? I cannot count the number of times I have heard people say, "I know what I believe. I don't need to write it down." This may very well be true, of course. But how many high school exams did I struggle through because I *thought* I knew the material and neglected to get it outside of myself to confirm such presumption? Many, particularly in physics. How often do we prefer the protected intimacy of our own head-knowledge, which simply protects us from the challenge of public or shared knowledge, perspectives we had not considered? Frequently. We often underestimate the human capacity for self-deception and avoidance of challenge. Conversing with small groups and engaging variously theological reading, however, will offer new considerations of other perspectives, or a process of moving from what some call an "embedded" perspective into a "deliberative" one. [24] An articulate voice requires an intentional wrestling with what lies implicit within you and what you have encountered or will encounter. Such articulation should not solidify theological wisdom for the rest of your life, or else it is questionably wisdom. Such writing should register your own claims and self-knowledge—personally authentic, studiously legitimated, and eventually traditionally grounded—resonant with some classical and contemporary theological perspectives and suggestive of your own participation within covenantal community processes. The act of writing especially offers gifts of awareness for those who do not consider themselves proficient at writing. The point, in the end, is not the prose, but the process-into-prose. Writing in a stilted fashion still allows others to love what is offered, prune what cannot grow, and nurture blossoms previously unseen. Ultimately, a written record of story into an artisanal theology offers a supple and compelling historical witness to the Story of God, the One who sustains and subverts "communities" yearning for community by enlivening "covenants" with continually renewed covenantal companionships.

FINAL PRELIMINARIES: TO BE (ORDAINED)
OR NOT TO BE (ORDAINED)?

A last word for those nudged into a consideration of ordained ministry today. This book will attune you to the delights and refining fires in store for you, found in the crucible of the discourses of academy–congregation–tradition. It considers the lived experiences of many as they entered into participation in larger, if not necessarily safe, communities of discernment. "Safe" communities—by which I mean those in which we may be wisely vulnerable—are harder to find today within ideologically polarized denominations and an increasingly legalistic culture. Admitting this overtly may be discomforting and threatening to some seasoned readers invested in larger systems of faithful discipleship. Any challenge of contemporary practices is often uncomfortable. As a matter of fact,

24. Stone and Duke, *How to Think Theologically*, 13–21.

well-trained and faithfully denominational or academic eyes *have* read a threat against received seminary education here, which is ironic.

First, all healthy institutions desire wizened and resilient leaders, which this approach promises to deliver in willing participants. Religious leadership will benefit greatly from the denominationally and academically shared goal of leadership formation through intentional formation in companionships that sustain vibrant faith. More personally, the felt-discomfort of wary eyes is ironic because my own vocational commitment lies within formal theological education. Theological education harbors the most plentiful resources and implicit communities within which I have found this sense of purpose and path of discipleship. All of us know that institutions of all kinds always require re-formation in order to stay vibrant, alive. This book simply aligns with that intent by offering a constructive *how* for practice. Institutions of theological education and denominations/traditions simply need to demonstrate more openness in the challenges of change, at least with respect to serving faith communities in leadership formation.

Perhaps you do *not* perceive an invitation into ordained ministry but clearly feel a passion and devotion for deeper discipleship through smaller communities of covenant. Listen to your instincts, in communion with your companions. Learn to distinguish between God's still, small voice for your own and your community's path and those voiced invitations made by faithful institutions whose purposes are larger but also potentially fragmenting of cherished companionships. If you have been gifted with a radically covenantal community of faith-practice already, do not leave it lightly. You may serve the relational wisdom of God's people, as a whole, *more* faithfully by continuing to deepen discipleship within such covenantal commitment. Engaging the fragmented and fragmenting disciplinary study within theological education as it is currently configured, at the expense of covenantal commitment lived into the world, may not be worth it. Do not underestimate the divide that happens, personally and systemically, when one becomes a "professional in ministry" in a larger tradition of faith. It is gift beyond measure, but not the *only* gift to be received, nor the only one that God grants for religious leadership.

Theological wisdom today promises more challenge and grace than words can express. As beloved strangers into God's new horizons, I suggest we give it welcome. How did Hamlet say it? "There are more things in heaven and earth . . . than are dreamt of in your philosophy." The Spirit loves each of us, equally fiercely, witnessed within scriptural testimony to covenantal belonging and within centuries of human companionship that continually urge us to greater awareness, deeper compassion, and stronger love. There is sustenance here for the world's deepest hungers. In shared commonalities and intimate yearnings, the path to spiritual maturity beckons to us all.

2

Community and Knowledge for an Intentional Formation

The word "community" does not mean today what it used to, nor do today's communities promise what has been assumed within it. Much of the past, particularly agricultural and early industrial eras, knew community to consist of locally-proximate persons who needed each other in order to survive.[1] The farming of produce complemented craftsmanship in town. Early practitioners of medicine, law, and education were often paid in agricultural or farming products. This was often called "payment in kind," which was rooted in a compassion, a kindness, which recognized diverse ways to match needs with whatever compensation was available. Physical subsistence actually depended upon such compassion. In contrast, today's cultural and socio-political environments rarely require neighbors to even meet one another, let alone face both delights and demands of a vibrant community life. Think of townhouse communities, for instance, or gated communities that share financial resources for facility maintenance yet have no other observably interpersonal life. Remember the steady disappearance of "the neighborhood," in both urban and suburban settings, due to mobility or increasing retail or heightened fear. Robert Putnam's sociological research in *Bowling Alone: the Collapse and Revival of American Community* led him to document and interpret increasing disconnection in the American public and the visible disintegration of social structures in civic life.[2] At the very least, the word "community" does not function as it has in previous eras. I therefore use "community," with quotation marks, to refer to a culturally conditioned sense, which is largely rhetorical. What we call "community" differs *sub-*

1. Myers, "Joy May End in Grief."
2. Putnam, *Bowling Alone: the Collapse and Revival of American Community*. See especially section II and chapter 15.

stantially from the biblical, theological, primarily relational phenomenon of community, assumed within historical, theological voices. For good and ill, "communities" today are unable to sustain previous practices and understandings of community.

A similar argument can be made about contemporary understandings of "covenant," which contrast with the vibrant phenomenon of belonging suggested in historical and scriptural witnesses. Christians attest to a covenantal identity concordant with Jews and Muslims as children of God's covenant(s) begun with Noah, Abraham and Sarah, and Moses. A renewed, transforming identity for Christians emerges within the life, death, and resurrection of Jesus of Nazareth, who spoke of a new covenant, sealed in his body and blood. Covenant in these traditions names the promises made by God to create, sustain, and redeem relationship, severed by humanity's recalcitrant will(s). Of course, humans still make "covenantal" promises.

And we break them, regularly, with awareness and without it. The most obvious one today is marriage, which falters regularly amidst job transitions, economic difficulties, human frailty, and more. Christian faith communities offer another instance of covenantal promise with the birth of a child whose parents bring him for the sacrament of baptism. The minister leads the congregation through the liturgy of covenantal promises made by God, by the congregation, by the parents to this child. Yet congregational members often repeat these words without much connected awareness for what it means actively to live into this commitment. How might they change their own lives and commitments, now to include additional behaviors or acts to be shaped by their covenantal promise? I even heard "covenant" used recently to describe one's commitment to exercise or health, in "my covenant with myself." There is no such thing as a privatized covenant! It is a primarily relational word that funds relationship with God and others through commitment, not self-will or autonomy. Finally, religious leadership formation occurs in covenant between local congregations, institutions of higher education, and national or denominational institutions. Yet there are more and more conditions placed upon who may be fostered within God's unconditional but demanding covenant—particularly around issues of human sexuality, gender, and ethnicity. God's mercifully just covenantal promises given witness in scripture rarely specify the details we consider crucial today, at least in the language and terminology we have available. Hebrew, Akkadian, Ugaritic, and *koiné* Greek—some of the biblical languages through which we receive our own English translations of scripture—simply do not offer conclusive, parallel meanings to modern languages. God's radically relational covenant with humanity challenges our conceptual categories, our "covenant," with a love and justice it seems we can only imagine.

GOD'S COVENANTAL COMMUNITY

In stark contrast, God's covenant is recognizable, if not reproducible, in a holy desire for intimacy, intent for reconciliation, holy anger, an invitation to union, a compassion for others. In smaller groups and within intentionally-covenantal companionships, a healthy and felt reality of this covenant still fires human awareness of God's relational primacy and a human interdependence. Covenant, without the quotation marks, is an irresistible claim and intentional commitment lived particularly into a life of faith and spiritual practice, known within a larger community story. This claim and commitment do not originate in personal choice, but participants do have completely free choice within it.

Covenant disrupts human life "as usual" and gives it deeper roots for discipleship than previously imaginable. It creates space in which intimate relationship grows, breathes, expands beyond the imagination of all parties. Not the other way around. Not willed relationships that we "work on" that then flower or blossom with God's love. Covenant enlivens the manner in which we perceive our worlds. It brings coherence into paradoxical or logically contradictory situations previously opaque to traditional theological understanding. It bears fruits of the Spirit, identifiable within scriptural witness. It also challenges previous scriptural understanding and places our story immediately, relationally, with those of present persons instead of past stories. Covenant is that kind of God-centered, committed companionship—holy friendship, discipleship groups, marriage, partnership, coaching, spiritual direction, and more—lived into real and regular time, with real people, who live the Life of God into particular stories. Covenantal companionship establishes the frames of reference within which theological understanding and interpretation develop toward wisdom to be lived, shared, celebrated. Ultimately, covenant returns each of us to an intensely intimate relationship and lived devotion to One who then returns us to our worlds in an overflowing delight and compassion to be shared with all.

In many North American contexts, delight within a covenantal community like this may be too much, too intimate, even too difficult for human individuals. It probably always has been without the threat of physical demise holding the dam together. Yet the graces and challenges of covenantal community offer precisely what many institutions of theological education strive to replicate within residential communities, assumed to be the best approach to theological education for leaders of future faith communities. Many institutions of contemporary theological education no longer have the financial or personal resources to create these residential communities, let alone authentically covenantal communities of belonging and maturation. Contemporary religious communities yearn for, fear, struggle to conceive this covenantal belonging for which human beings were created.

Our language, knowledge, even our fear gets in the way. We read the words relationship and community, yet know a media-saturated, warm-fuzzy intimacy and a commodification of community. To belong within a "community" today requires a cultural or psychological similarity, confirmed in voluntary choices or personal preference. We say covenant, but really mean a contract, with our commitment conditioned upon others' frailties.[3] We read about community yet struggle to face the self-knowledge and relational truth-telling that covenant promises. Given this, how could we have known that authentic intimacy is for the courageous of heart and requires covenantal commitment before it gets spiritually hot?[4] A web of human interdependence in which humans recognize themselves on common ground across the globe is literally inconceivable to most of us with an American self-sufficiency. A manner of living in which the heart of compassion grows and hurts alongside human ignorance, neglect, and suffering seems a fool's errand, because it is all so overwhelming. Yet within this heart of compassionate companionship lie seeds of delight, wonder, and love stronger than death, if we enter into it. It is not macabre or masochistic, but the hidden secret of a *living* faith tradition.

---

3. Volf, *Exclusion and Embrace*, 147.

4. Schnarch, *Passionate Marriage*, 100ff. See also Hilsman, *Intimate Spirituality*, 103ff, though his language centers in sacramentality, not explicitly covenantal language, per se.

Established institutions of theological education today offer the necessary depth and breadth for traditionally-rooted practices of faith, which are a crucial key to any living theological tradition. They are no more immune from today's "community" and "covenant" tensions, however. Unbeknownst to many, they do not necessarily offer the covenantal companionships and relational guidance for the shared theological wisdom in which spiritual practice deepens toward delight and risked compassion. The incredibly complex institutional ecology—numerous kinds of congregations, denominations, interfaith traditions, and specialized theological disciplines—insures that any one institution of theological education or spiritual resourcing could never provide one kind of religious identity or one kind of path. Exploring and harvesting the resources available within this overwhelming diversity of materials therefore requires a deeper understanding and willing acceptance of the governing worlds in which participants live, act, and discern their way.

GOVERNING "WORLDS"

An interdisciplinary team of scholars has provided a helpful way to think about how someone can navigate social systems and personal identity, each with an eye toward the other.[5] In their view, each of us lives in multiple socio-cultural worlds, all of which impose assumed identities onto individuals and groups. As every seasoned religious leader knows, and as I tell my students regularly, "You will be many things to many people, which can be a blessing if you know who and whose you are, or a curse, if you do not know or have forgotten." Multiple worlds, multiple identities—or what Holland et al. call *identities-in-practice*.[6] Yet this term also suggests that each of us receives a capacity for action, which is more developed in some than in others. Every world and situation offers an unavoidable "self-authoring" in which we either act with or against the imposed identities. Understanding persons and actions within this notion of multiple worlds requires observation and exploration that assumes two things: one, each person has at least some human agency in every situation, and two, each person is being uncontrollably shaped by unseen forces of their socio-cultural worlds. Although one can describe many more worlds at play within established institutions of theologi-

5. Holland et al., *Identity and Agency in Cultural Worlds*, 49ff.
6. Holland et al., 270–87.

cal education, three primary ones stand out immediately: the academy, the local congregation, and the national/international denomination or tradition.

In order to excel at teaching, researching, writing, or tradition-ing the wisdom of previous generations, theological faculty must excel within their own world of the academy. We are formed in critical, rigor-ous, and historical doctoral programs steeped in Enlightenment habits of mind—healthy skepticism (what is often called a hermeneutics of suspicion) and abilities for imaginative and daring deconstruction-re-construction of traditional ideas of faith, scripture, theology, etc. Highly respected scholars exhibit a command of their disciplinary literature, a highly-literate finesse with prose and quantitative studies, and an analyti-cal argumentation of precise scholarship for their discipline, or the com-munity of scholars or guild. And what a contribution to knowledge such highly literate finesse provides! What contagious passion for the texts of God and the traditions within and beyond that the Holy has moved for centuries! There is little more compelling than a human being gifted with precise analytical skills, devoting herself to a deeper and deeper under-standing of what God is about in this world. It takes courage to move be-yond socially-limited human imagination. It takes trust to delve into the doubt-encrusted, diamond-worthy Reality of Spirit. It takes true desire to sustain this courage and doubt all the way through to God's ongoing creation of reconciliation, wholeness, grace.

Another incredibly diverse world at play in the pursuit of deeper spiritual practice can be that of the local congregation. Congregations come in wildly different shapes and sizes, from older (and mostly small-er) mainline communities steeped in theological and cultural practices of modernity to so-called megachurches or Pentecostal congregations finding new centers of gravity in global mission and contemporary ex-plorations of expressed needs. Practicing congregations are breaking traditional molds of what it means to be historically rooted and vibrant within faith mission.[7] Internet cohorts of seekers are finding intermit-tent yet disciplined ways of gathering for worship and renewing urban centers of need.[8] Amidst this multi-religious and multi-form landscape, radically covenantal communities of historical witness and presumption

7. Butler-Bass, *Practicing Congregation*, 79–90.

8. See, for example, Kimball, *Emerging Church*.

have all but disappeared, although remnants and descriptions remain. In their place are voluntary, institutionalized, potentially polarized gatherings presumed to be "church" or "synagogue" or "mosque" in outdated forms, buildings, habits. Even so, what remarkable witness such voluntary gatherings of faithful disciples can offer a community facing increased homelessness, poverty, illness, and injustice. What gifts of God are discovered and renewed amidst "ordinary life" in such a community of disciples. What remarkable stewardship of theological traditions in the most intimate of relationships, in child-like adult encounters with the Sacred, in education and discernment of identity as a people of God. Thomas Hawkins speaks of the "whitewater world of change" facing local congregations and smaller faith communities today.[9] No wonder there is both an unsteadiness *and* real potential about what it means to be faithfully local and globally aware as a local congregation today.

A third governing world for any pursuit of deeper spiritual practice and shared theological wisdom comes from the gathered and dispersed communities of denomination or faith tradition, the interconnected and national/international institutional structures that retain vertical or hierarchical flows of money and power, and largely approve or certify the formation of religious leadership today (among many other missions, of course). Some representatives within these structures serve faithfully to mend historically broken relationships between the diverse traditions of the communities of God. Some reach out to peripheral populations because they are free from local misperceptions and geographical closeness that may prevent seeing a mission opportunity. Others sustain the tradition's identity amidst a broader culture that holds professed holiness or theology in some disdain. It is a difficult and necessary calling to give witness to those who hunger yet cannot see what God promises in historical particularities of lived traditions. The local congregation is related to these structures, but often only in the person of the pastor/rabbi/imam, the ministry professional. The academy is related to these structures, as it is a collaborative partner in the preparation of leadership. Yet these denominational or institutional bodies are the ones perceivably, publicly responsible for certification in the practice of ministry in a professional sense.

9. Hawkins, *Learning Congregation*, 3–4.

Given the diversity of worlds—even beyond the minimal three described here—it takes quite a balancing act to know who and whose you are, in any given situation of intimate inquiry or religious ministry. We have little control over how our worlds shape us and try to tell us who we are. Much of the time, it feels we have little capacity for actions that can counteract this outside shaping, that can give each of us choice in who we may become. One quintessentially biblical and theological world *does* offer a worldview and a disciplined practice that promises a startling, liberating path amidst other worlds, which easily contradict and conflict with each other but yet may find their fullest expressions in the end.

SPIRITUAL STEWARDSHIP

Spiritual stewardship names the figured world within which a two-fold logic or pattern guides intentional participation in shaping oneself and being shaped by others. A *steward* is one who does not govern nor own the household, yet is responsible for its internal domestic affairs. He is responsible, yet not ultimately responsible. She is able to act within her sphere of responsibility, yet is impotent to determine how her actions will be received or how they will contribute to the larger community. Risk is unavoidable. Trust becomes a lived practice of affirmation *and* betrayal. Stewardship therefore refers to service, but an important distinction arises here for spiritual stewardship. Spiritual stewardship describes service that *sustains* self and others. How often are religious leaders able to ask and answer for themselves, in the affirmative: Does this calling sustain my deepest passions? It is *that* kind of service that shapes and nourishes all participants through self-assertion and choice, through surrender and devotion, ultimately to the uncontrollable Holy. Relationship forms the heart of this world mutually negotiated and freely configured by those who know who (and whose) they are, as well as their own limitations and talents. Stewardship configures relationship that is not only sustained but celebrated regardless of theological persuasion, cognitive gifting, or access to cultural and material resources.

Most importantly, the world of spiritual stewardship creates and recreates, through its constitutive relationality,[10] a deeper logic than those of achievement, mastery, expertise, and professional excellence. The lived realities of radical suffering, injustice, poverty, war, loss, disease,

10. See Loder and Neidhardt, *The Knight's Move.*

and death are not denied, nor are they neglected. These realities simply do not determine the God-centered relationship lived outward into community. Nor can such realities ultimately destroy such relationship within global communities of faith. A *disciplined* spiritual stewardship names the responsible and responsive life possible within established institutions of theological education and given shape by this logic of stewardship. Accountable, spiritual practices within smaller communities of covenantal commitment and mutual discernment offer both intentional human agency and covenantal shaping of those practices. It is this worldview, embodied with covenantal and accountable spiritual practice, which then sustains a kind of knowing that is primarily communal and suited to the pursuits of shared theological wisdom.

UNPREDICTABLE KNOWING TOWARD WISDOM

Living theological traditions promise a deeper way of knowing in community and its human frailty, given historical witness over centuries of God's people who have bridged texts and traditions too diverse to name. This unpredictable way of knowing roots persons in living traditions in order to liberate human spirits and manifest divine grace. It frees all of us in the academy, the local congregation, and the denomination/tradition to delve deeply into the mysteries of God with a patience and gentleness born of deeper sight and received compassion from others. We face discomfort in caring challenges against staid notions of church or synagogue or mosque, often grown fearful of change. We find previously known or frail ideas of grace, mercy, anger, and justice expanded beyond our imaginations into renewed grace, mercy, anger, and justice. With a tenacity of spirit and mind, we engage a disciplined spiritual stewardship that can form not only what we come to know, but how, communally, it makes sense within our own story (and traditions) as well as those around us. We need "the other" for this kind of wisdom. We need a willingness to face discomfort if knowledge is to serve toward shared delight.

Take, for example, a traditional Jewish rabbi entering a Roman Catholic church, a context previously disavowed by many in his worshipping community.[11] Traditional Jews are not allowed to enter a church within their communal norms, let alone sit in a pew and observe the sights and smells—an open-hearted Jesus on the cross, heavy incense,

11. Kula, *Yearnings*, 19.

stained glass windows, candles burning. Yet for some reason, he entered. He sat there for a while, though he wanted nothing more than to leave. Then he found himself thinking, "What if my heart was that open? What if I could feel everyone's pain, so much so that my heart exploded?" In a startling moment, he understood a shared meaning of sacred heart between two traditions often at odds with one another. He heard the words from a prayer he'd said every day since he was young, in a whole new way: "'Karov YHWH L'nishberai Lev,' God is Close to the Brokenhearted."[12] He found—received, actually—a new and powerful way to live into his own tradition *and* know God is bigger than he had previously imagined. This insight required a willingness to face discomfort and a whole other community, however—other people, other symbols, other practices.

Then there is the Lukan story within scriptural witness (Luke 24:13–35). Two men on the road to Emmaus are discussing what they know, what they have seen, their sadness or anger at the events of the now-called Passion weekend. They meet the Stranger who begins to teach them what they thought they already knew, inflaming their hearts with the ways of God yet unseen, written yet not understood. They share table fellowship. Their eyes are opened. They see. Then they do not see. Jesus, the Stranger become familiar, vanishes. We hear the disciples' excitement as they return to proclaim what they have learned, what they have seen, and then what they did not see. Any pursuit of deeper spiritual practice must be like this. Theological education at its best is like this: seeing the Stranger become familiar, then un-seeing all over again in order to see anew in the future. Wise ones who have traveled their paths before us remind us again and again: as soon as you know for certain who God is or what your faith tradition is, what religious ministry is, then you lose the ability to see more than that moment and how well it fits in with what you already know.

Earlier in the narrative, Simon Peter also had to see, then un-see; know, then un-know. He hears his rabbi ask, "Who do you say that I am?" Probably with not a little fear, he steps forward, "You are the Messiah, the son of the Living God" (Matt 16:16). For such seeing faith, he receives a new name, Peter, the Rock—an intimate act of naming, and testimony to a new covenant grafted into an older one. He has seen and knows. Not two verses later, we learn that Peter's idea of the Messiah has little to do

12. Ibid.

with God's actual intention. No conquering leader, liberating the people from Roman oppression. No divine trumpet signaling an overt revolution. A suffering servant. Death on a cross. Rising again. Appearing to the disciples and then vanishing again. Peter's faithful yet ultimately idolatrous idea of the Messiah causes his rabbi to say, "Get behind me Satan!" We often misremember that Simon Peter was being faithful to his tradition *and* he had only received a portion of what he needed to know. We always only have a portion in order to be faithful to what is next, who we are to be now. Good and faithful practice, undergirded by a liberating theological wisdom, is just like that, regardless of tradition: faithful and incomplete, seen-known and yet unseen-unknown.

Trappist monk and contemplative, Thomas Keating, also offers a glimpse of this from within Sufism, a mystical strand of Islam.

> A Sufi master had lost the key to his house and was looking for it in the grass outside. He got down on his hands and knees and started running his fingers through every blade of grass. Along came eight or ten of his disciples. They said, "Master, what is wrong?" He said, "I have lost the key to my house." They said, "Can we help you find it?" He said, "I would be delighted." So they all got down on their hands and knees and started running their fingers through the grass. As the sun grew hotter, one of the more intelligent disciples said, "Master, have you any idea where you might have lost the key?" The Master replied, "Of course, I lost it in the house." To which they all exclaimed, "Then why are we looking for it out here?" He said, "Isn't it obvious? There is more light here."[13]

A Sufi master is well-familiar with insight-unseen, knowledge-unknown. At some level, he knows where the lost key is: in the house. He unknows it enough to invite his disciples into the search where knowledge is to be found: where the light is. He sees because of the light, but he also unsees because the key is within the house, where there is less light, if any at all. You hear his delight, his sharing of the search, his willingness to be with his disciples as the sun grew hotter, and his easy answer with an impish smile, upon the question of one of the more intelligent disciples.

One point of the story is the key within us, lost and to be found, through light and shadow in a search shared in community. We begin with self-images and ideas important to who we are and what we need,

13. Keating, *The Human Condition*, 8–9.

and then we must just as faithfully release some of them. Our ideas are only the beginning, to be shared within an inquiring community. We explore the right questions, which then become the old questions. We need to have our eyes opened, knowing full well that sight only goes so far. A theological education for the pursuit of wisdom is where the light is, but the institutions that help us search in community are not necessarily where we find the key. They give opportunities to find the key, but only when there is willingness to sustain ambiguity, to encounter conflict, to trust beyond a perceived ability to do so, and ultimately maintain a vision of hope for what a living and unpredictable God was, is, will be.

All of us pursue our yearnings for God with unavoidable preconceptions and uncertainties, not only about who we are but who the church expects us to be in the future. It is a human inevitability that is actually the seed of grace for true learning within the Holy. Pursuit of theological study usually results from one of three things: a compelling conviction, a mystical-transcendent encounter, or a quest for the meaningful. Yet rarely do we get an uncomplicated assurance of our conviction, a conclusive explanation of such an encounter, *or* a satisfying completion of such a quest. Conviction, encounter, and quest are nouns that should connote continuous movement rather than stasis.

This ambiguity, desire, and openness to wrestling with the Holy promises unexpected insight and deep joy. Deeper spiritual practice, as a received and God-given activity, grows as a grace born within you, fully yours but not of your creation. To be wholly other, it cannot be what you imagined. To be what God promises within a world of observable suffering, it necessarily contains promise and suffering, celebration and shared sorrow. Deep joy has an intimate knowledge of both. No institution can prepare you for this kind of learning, nor does any certification or theological degree insure that you will participate in it.

This kind of knowing is a lightly held wisdom born of formation and personal integration. It is not an objective knowledge obtained for professional certification, achievement of academic excellence, or successful completion of all ordination requirements. It is the holy grail of all those institutions or faith communities who yearn to prepare persons for religious service and leadership. It is the one thing that many institutions and well-trained theological leaders today are adversely formed to tradition or emulate. Institutions are human collectives with a systemic force and power of their own. Leaders (including myself) have been formed in a highly critical, literate form of knowledge, understanding, and interpretation. Personal integration toward a relational wisdom, on the other hand, moves with a more subtle, immediate force of its own. The relational way of wisdom originates within one-on-one companionships and cohort-group covenantal relationships. It is the continuing oral truth of a living tradition that gets handed from body to body, person to person, not text to text. This way of knowing happens within theological institutions today, but it is also becoming an increasingly implicit curriculum.[14] Theological education, as formally conceived, requires renewed, explicit attention to a participatory, embodied formation and integration. Sustaining this lightly-held knowledge unto wisdom is only given practical shape in a disciplined spiritual stewardship, which urges each governing world toward its fullest expression in service of the whole.

DISCIPLINED SPIRITUAL STEWARDSHIP: GIFTS AND PRACTICES FOR UN/KNOWING TOWARD WISDOM

Disciplined spiritual stewardship describes accountable and covenantal spiritual practices necessary to foster such a lightly held yet intimately costly wisdom within the expansive world of spiritual stewardship. It begins with the Holy-given gift of humility. This term does not mean, as Roberta Bondi observes, "a continuous cringing, cultivating a low self-imagine and taking a perverse pleasure in being always forgotten, unnoticed, or taken for granted."[15] In its ancient sense, and as it is intended here, humility is primarily a relational term, motivated by the law in service of love, not guilt or shame or even a willful self-sacrifice. It is "an attitude of heart" without which virtues have no faithful context. It is difficult and calls for the renunciation of all that the modern world holds dear: material prosperity, advancement, satisfaction of desires at the expense of others, right to dominate.[16] Humility, therefore, cannot be humanly achieved, though it can be received in an active openness to "the other,"

---

14. Eisner, *The Educational* Imagination, 88–89. This submersion into implicit curriculum proceeds logically from an increasingly legal culture that limits deeper relationships for unfortunate as well as good reasons, e.g., protection against harassment, misconduct, and more; the assessment of outcomes requiring more quantitative articulations, etc.

15. Bondi, *To Love as God Loves*, 18.

16. Ibid., 54.

to God—or in non-theistic view, compassion-wisdom-knowledge. Being open to others requires a risked vulnerability, healthily chosen with curious willingness. This vulnerability is not a virtue in itself, but a path to deepened awareness, healthy relationship, and encounter. It offers avenue to healthy relationships that sustain self and others. Vulnerability also entails risk of injury, of course, but injuries that can be stewarded wisely for greater understanding and unexpected compassion. The problem in theological education, of course, is that no one can teach humility. One receives it, or models it. Even so, skills and practices—deep listening, covenantal belonging, spiritual practices centered in silence—can create intentionally, healthily vulnerable space within which receptivity grows. This space I am calling the figured world of spiritual stewardship.

Humility, openness, and being opened result in a learned, deep listening, or what Emma Justes calls *hearing beyond the words*. Organized by the four core qualities of hospitality—vulnerability, humility, thoughtful availability, and reciprocity—deep listening shapes the communal and most intimate parts of the human condition shared. "We all have in common the human experiences of pain, suffering, fear, loss, and joy—every human emotion."[17] Walter Brueggemann, for this reason, names listening to be a discipline of humanness or obedience.[18] It requires time, patience, commitment to understanding, and awareness of communication patterns with loving-kindness held intentionally in mind. Being claimed within God's love appears at the front to be a comforting answer to prayer—which it often is—but its vibrant mutuality also elicits a receptivity and responsiveness that are threatening nonetheless. Deep listening changes the listener, not necessarily the one talking or the situation of shared suffering or joy.

Covenantal belonging—independent of the social categories of marriage, union, romance, or sexual identities—requires such listening, through discomfort into new insights and deepened intimacy. Yet neither does covenantal belonging originate with the human will or congregational membership. Such belonging grows in interpersonal intimacies amidst a shared, relational willingness to surrender primarily to God/Compassion, then to oneself, then to another human being in holy friendship. Submission to any work that the Holy may have in mind

17. Justes, *Hearing Beyond the Words*, 95.
18. Brueggemann, *Theology of the Old Testament*, 460.

requires little surrenders like these to pave the way beyond any previously conceived goals or achievements. Ironically, faith communities with more hierarchical, episcopal polities do tradition such practices of submission to the Holy, even as lived expressions of these practices can be abusive or seem counter-culturally authoritarian, inappropriate to an authentically vibrant, liberating relationship with God.

Sustained spiritual disciplines of all kinds inform and reform the world of spiritual stewardship in particular lives, thereby invigorating participation in formation with grace and fidelity to who and what one values. Particularly for those in deeper theological study of texts, an intentional return to quiet practices—like meditation, *lectio divina*, and contemplation—is fundamental, if implausible within current institutional ecologies. Words and conceptual thought for speaking fill the worlds of theological education, often hiding the necessary self-awareness and relational lessons to be learned in centering into one's mind-chatter, to be quieted for a lived wisdom. An unspoken space or inarticulate immediacy, silence cannot be conceptually or linguistically controlled. It can only be interrupted. In situations tinged heavily by professionalism, mastery, expertise, and achievement, silence is the only tactical response to the human misconceptions about power amidst divine and compassionate tasks. Spiritual disciplines, especially those centered in silence and truly indwelt in communities of radical covenant, ultimately communicate God's interconnection of conceivable and inconceivable diversity within creation and beyond.

No less important for a disciplined spiritual stewardship are purposeless, spontaneous practices of play.[19] Religious folks can be the most serious, dignified, and constraining people, out of touch with the risk of personal creativity that resembles risks of faith. Religious leaders have the difficulty of living at the serious crossroads of life—death, disease, poverty, injustice, and more—all of which can plant a messianic seriousness difficult to release.[20] Playfulness therefore becomes even more important. How else to remember in tactile ways what a gift it is to be a child of God? Much of contemporary congregational life focuses on the habits of identifiable traditions necessary to sustain familiar identity amidst great change. Understandable, but not very conducive to receiving new gifts of

19. Koppel, "Pastoral Theological Reflection on Play in the Ministry," 3–12.
20. See also Hess, "Sabbath Renewal: Recovering Play in Pastoral Ministry," 15.

membership, imagination, a shared delight that empowers and companions others. Practices of play—truly spontaneous ways of being together, not privatized entertainment or fellowship—reform communities and trust for God's greater adventures.[21]

Finally, a disciplined spiritual stewardship requires time and space, unfilled and fallow, which can be rare in institutions of theological learning. Why the fallow space? Unfilled, perceivably empty space shows the highest form of praise as well as a reliance upon God as primary actor, teacher, companion, judge. Empty space often reminds over-busy ministers of their finitude and limitation, not as a character flaw to be addressed but a cherished fact of being a creature within God's primary care. Waiting in defiance of one's own felt-schedule shows an open-hearted willingness to receive, not willfulness to impose. Fallow and peripheral time opens a space for unexpected encounters and flexible listening. The Zen master pours a cup of tea for an experienced student who is seeking wisdom through the master's teaching. The master pours until the cup is full, and then continues to pour tea, overflowing onto the saucer and the table and the floor. The student cries out for him to stop. "Likewise," the master replies, "How can you hear what I have to say if you are already so full?" Ultimately, intentional formation requires commitment to fallow space and peripheral times informally honored within a covenantal community. Such spaciousness promises a deeper wisdom born in relationship and created in God's time.

In this fashion, those who pursue deeper spiritual practice gain the necessary perspectives and lived-but-written experience of those whom God has loved before they were born. Generations of historical witness give texture and contour to theological worlds become stale without vibrant human breath and action. God's mercies and actions become more mysterious, more wonderful, more startling in their historical reality. Humanity's propensity for self-ignorance, suffering, and the injury of others becomes a more urgent impetus for deeper discipleship and life in a living God, who can and does redeem such things for those who love. At the same time, truly entering into formation within established institutions of theological education will develop habits of mind that can objectify or dissect a relational knowing of intimate integrity. Knowledge may often be pursued for the sake of knowledge, not for the sake of

21. See also Berryman, *Godly Play.*

compassion or deeper discipleship or service. It is crucial to sense the difference.

Critical thinking that provides an objective distance does offer an important capacity to question thoughts from their founding assumptions, which are often plain wrong, injurious, or inaccurate within broader communal knowing. Critical reflection corrects false assumptions—including prejudices and fideism unworthy of a loving Creator—toward *tested* truths, resilient and verifiable by others over time within broader communities of belonging. These habits of mind bring a more reflective practitioner, a more spiritually resilient and awakened leader, into the religious shaping of faith communities. But such habits—the root of our conundrum, actually—just as easily tradition a way of knowing that divides communities, isolates humans from themselves and others, and eventually a living God. Knowledge for the sake of knowledge will divide and conquer. Knowledge rooted in a pre-emptive love—critically chosen and willing to exist in a place of unknowing—promises a deeper life in God, for the other, in the world..

Let us be prepared, however. Here is where we hear some talk about a potential "loss of faith."[22] Releasing treasured ideas to love another until you know together, intimately, your commonalities and differences—that is a threatening idea for many. But is a faith that can be lost worth keeping? What kind of faith was it, if it was so rigidly pre-defined that God's expanse could not form it anew, breathe new life into the daily dyings of finite creatureliness? Was it truly faith if the exercise of personal will and certitude could drown out God's still, small voice urging more awareness, more compassion, stronger love? I suspect that claims of lost faith were actually, for whatever reason, lives full of religiosity but without faith from the very beginning. A critical, listening faith will be supple, reformed, and continually reforming, shaped in a manner that the Spirit desires for callings into deeper discipleship. A living faith embodies a radical trust in situations through which God can do the works of unmerited grace and compassion.

---

22. Pope Benedict XVI and Henry Taylor, *Truth and Tolerance: Christian Belief and World Religions*, 133. They cite an author, Kriele, *Anthroposophie and Kirche*, especially a chapter on "Loss of Faith through Theology." Other voices name this fear, with good reason, in face of vastly different epistemological and communal values than those prescribed within the secular or empiricist-favored fields of university discourse.

Therefore, bearers of living wisdom follow its path through receiving new perspectives and wrestling with old ones. This wrestling only happens faithfully when sustained by communities of belonging. Consider the relationships in which you are coming to know a theological wisdom. What fruits of the Spirit do you observe? Is the knowledge leading toward wholeness, a deep delight, and a compassionate service of the other and world? Is there a twinkle in the eye of the faculty person who clearly knows a deeper delight than he can articulate? Even in the overworked weariness of Americans today, is there a passion that is contagious for the good gifts of God? *Those* fruits will contextualize any and all critical coursework toward the tasks of integration and relationally-whole knowing so necessary today for shaping faith communities.

CONCLUSION

Community and covenant must meet one another again, however difficult American individualism and self-sufficiency make that for the world. People drawn to wisdom traditions will continue to pursue deeper knowledge through whatever resources are made available to them in theological education for the practice of ministry. Living a relational wisdom today, however, requires facing the felt-conundrum that specialized expertise both clarifies traditional knowledge and under-nourishes its interpersonal roots in covenant for a life in God, for the other, in the world. Intentional formation promises a deeper, more integrated way of knowing within covenantal, intimate relationship. Its objectives can be articulated and engaged. Assessment and achievement is quantifiable only within an overwhelmingly complex, institutional, and interpersonal collaboration between worlds of the academy, local congregation, and theological tradition. Dissatisfaction is assured, undeniable, to be expected. Imagination and satisfaction come, however, when intentional formation is rooted in a disciplined spiritual stewardship, guided by a two-sided logic of stewardship and resonant with the ambivalent experience of shaping-and-being-shaped. Delight comes.

The *how* of all this begins to take concrete shape in the various practices of storying and being storied by others. Personal stories, intertwined with God's and God's peoples' stories, are paramount for persons becoming wise to their own gifts, shadows, purpose, mutually discerned within real communities of faith. An ability to surrender to God's presence while attending to communally theological and historical pasts, crafts personal story both as intimately instructive and communally shaped. Personal stories are never completely personal, in other words, but become story only within webs of other stories. Lived interdependence matures personal story beyond a privatism, however. What is a most intimate gift especially for one person propels, with great care, God's grace for the benefit of all. Personal stories undergird this way of knowing, therefore, only by being shared outward with skill and care. They form deeply intimate, covenantal community in this careful and caring movement outward. In the storying and being storied that results, God's living Story erupts as and when God desires, woven into previously unfathomable purposes. Scriptural witness, historical tradition, and communal discernment all help us hear the Story and *participate* in it. Storying like this reforms and transforms intentional participants with a living theological wisdom, which God has chosen as receptacle for the Story that saves us all.

3

Practicing Into Wisdom-Knowing:
Personal and Communal Stories in Covenantal Community

There is great irony in Westernized, self-obsessed cultures that simultaneously prevent a deepening awareness or awakening of the self to the complexities and delights of the human condition. Natalie Goldberg calls this lack of awareness alienation, from self and from others. Mother Teresa observed it as a brand of American poverty called loneliness.[1] I think both terms are descriptive. In contrast to "cultural force" interpretations, however, the reality has just as much to do with the overwhelming energy required to author oneself, to be continually responsive to one's environment, to awaken again and again. Awakening is painful, after all. Seeing things you have not seen before, knowing your own weaknesses alongside your favorable self-images, requires a responsiveness (or unconscious avoidance) and the recognition that you missed something now so apparent. Ouch. Deepening spiritual practice requires a willingness to awaken, lived in a surrender to the discomfort such awakening heightens. Theological wisdom grows only in the deep listening to others with their (perhaps) absolute convictions you know to be faulty or at least only partial. This chapter introduces a storying way of knowing through practices of spiritual autobiography and shared reflections within covenantal groups. The purpose is to facilitate awakening in deeper spiritual practice and the pursuit of wisdom, and the path is primarily communal. It begins concretely by delving into one's own stories, amidst the stories of others, within intentionally covenantal companionship.

Perhaps unbeknownst to many, this path has deeply theological roots. Protestant Reformer John Calvin begins his famous *Institutes of the Christian Religion* with an epistemological observation for the pursuit

1. Goldberg, *Long Quiet Highway*, 25.

of wisdom. "Nearly all the wisdom we possess, that is to say, true and sound and wisdom, consists of two parts: the knowledge of God and of ourselves."[2] Without the knowledge of self, there is no knowledge of God; without the knowledge of God, there is no knowledge of self. Now, we live in an era of apparent and overflowing knowledge, made accessible to more and more of us through digital resources, global media, and a heightened prevalence of literacy and education. It is easy to assume, then, that knowledge has deepened about both humanity and God, even their interrelationship. Knowing the scriptures more, with more translations, should mean we know better who God is. Scientific knowledge, having access to specialized and well-researched perspectives on all aspects of the human condition, should result in greater knowledge about human persons. Ironically, the overflow of information results in much less personal and communal awareness, from too much knowledge, too many perspectives, and little sense of how to digest it all toward wisdom and compassionate decision-making. Knowledge is often refused entrance into our being, into our bones, with this overwhelm of commentary. In contrast, the kind of knowledge that comes from within and beyond the self in an enacted performance of meaning requires what George Steiner calls an answerability, an authentic understanding or a "responding responsibility," a knowledge or learning by heart that affords an "indwelling clarity and life-force."[3] Calvin's use of knowledge signals just this distinction, which is why he is quoted by so many.

Calvin interrelates the knowledge of God and the knowledge of self through an *existential apprehension*, not purely objective knowledge or theological expertise. Calvin's use of the Latin *cognitio* and *notitia*, translated into the French *cognoissance*, refers to this existential apprehension of God and human self, interrelated and known, each to the other, through revelation. Related words he uses include *agnitio*, recognition or acknowledgement, and *intelligentia*, meaning perception. The knowledge of God can never be a purely objective phenomenon accessed from information and available resources, even including the spectacles of scripture.[4] It comes within apprehension: a deepened awareness, discomforting perception, and willing recognition of the human self, by itself.

2. Calvin, *Institutes of the Christian Religion*, 35.

3. Steiner, *Real Presences*, 8–9.

4. Battle, Translator's Commentary to Calvin, *Institutes of the Christian Religion*, 35 n. 1.

Self- and God-knowledge become revealed through an embodied know-ing received from practices of piety, trust, and reverence.[5] If you desire to know God, you must enter into existential apprehension in which God and self somehow both become revealed, revelatory, recognized. A good portion of formal theological studies focuses upon the historical and theo-logical texts of God's witnesses. If Calvin is right, these will be naught but straw unless you face yourself squarely, within a covenantal community of confidentiality and challenge. Well-felt apprehension, then, is sure to follow. This path of knowing requires much more personal and integra-tive rigor than could ever be articulated easily in religious or theological prose today.

BELONGING, RELATIONSHIP, TRANSFORMATION

"Storying and being storied" represents one of the oldest manners of hu-man knowledge transmission that we know. My family's way of being family formed this in me from early childhood, as my grandmother told stories, again and again. My father tells stories, again and again. Pretty soon, I suppose I will too. "That reminds me of a story . . ." is a delightfully inescapable entry in my family lexicon. Our stories regale listeners with antics of uncles when they were young, old jokes that become one-lin-ers of intimate reference, points of poignant events in the larger history of relationships. Few (if any) of these stories suggest historical genius or brilliant originality, such that they deserve memory for posterity in the human race. Yet the stories formed my earliest sense of self, family, belonging, and possibility. Also my sense of humor. The shift to storied knowing from a historical or objective knowledge requires seeing the wisdom way of personal stories becoming communal belonging.

Knowing stories and being able to tell them in the right way, at the right time, signals a web of belonging deeper than words. Stories root personal belonging, but not as we consider it in much of North America today. Our modern to postmodern cultures encourage us to favor a de-tached and so-called objective approach to our world. Belonging today ap-pears to require knowing the most precise, correct version of stories, with the right details argued from the right sources. The story itself—whatever it may be, whether it is the war, the Bible, national history, or race—has become a war zone of who said what with which credible evidence sup-

5. Calvin, *Institutes of the Christian Religion*, 39–43.

porting one's claims. Stories like this come from a modern worldview, unraveling in postmodern critiques.[6] This mind-set—what some call the "technological mind"[7] within an "economic consumerism"[8]—objectifies something in order to devote it to some other purpose, with some other layered significance.

It takes a new frame of reference for most of us today to realize that the story-telling is not always about the story. Stories are not only about the plot, form, and function—object lessons with propositional lessons to be memorized. They are an entrance into a larger frame of meaning and web of relationships that constitute personal identities. They have just as many implicit and explicit dimensions as those who tell them—individuals and social networks alike. Harvard anthropology professor Michael Jackson pushes this individual-social frame even further with an exploration of Hannah Arendt's view: "storytelling is never simply a matter of creating either personal or social meanings, but an aspect of "the subjective in-between" in which a multiplicity of private and public interests are always problematically in play."[9] Stories share, indirectly and through their telling, a community's sense of love, propriety, value, humor, and particularity. Stories remind listeners of where they came from, who belongs with whom, and what kinds of behaviors are understood in which ways. Storytelling establishes boundaries and then just as easily challenges and transgresses them within the creative call of a narrative.[10] They do not exist for themselves, but for the telling and hearing and telling again that signal a shared relationship, a shared history of belonging or antagonism or both, over time. To belong, you must know the gist of the story but you can tell it with your own twist, at the right times, within a broader frame of reference almost intuited by others with whom you belong. Herbert Anderson and Edward Foley bring this co-creative storytelling into the interconnection between human and divine narratives as well. They examine a reciprocity between storytelling and ritual that "enhances the possibility of weaving human and divine stories into a single fabric."[11] Not only do stories shape human belonging, they can

---

6. Grenz, *Primer on Post-Modernism*; Bernstein, *Beyond Objectivism and Relativism*.

7. Loder and Neidhardt, *Knight's Move*, 6.

8. Miller, *Consuming Religion*.

9. Jackson, *Politics of Storytelling*, 11.

10. Ibid., 25.

11. Anderson and Foley, *Mighty Stories, Dangerous Rituals*, 36ff.

connect God and humanity, heaven and earth, in a "spirituality of reconciliation"[12] in which storytelling and rituals facilitate wholeness and
interdependence.

Stories thereby establish relationship in an intentional willingness
to listen, even through difficulty or difference. The blending of family
loyalties within any new marriage, for instance, will show a negotiation of
family stories, acceptable behaviors, and unmet expectations. It took me
two years into my marriage to realize that Minnesotans have very definite
(and repetitive, I might add) patterns of politeness such as the "invitation-decline, invitation-decline, invitation-acceptance" requirement. It is
considered rude to accept a gift on the first offer, I now know. My family
expected you to say what you wanted and happily receive whatever might
be offered, on the first offer. I was apparently "rude" in my new blend of
storying, for two whole years, before I learned that difference. Listening
to the Maguire stories over these several years has allowed me to live into
a deeper relationship, simply in the telling, hearing, listening, and learning. I am now a Hess and a Maguire, but the stories of one family remain
distinct from the stories of the other. Relationship grows in the sustained
acts of storying amidst difference, which can be unavoidably complex.

Each of us is born into an unchosen, given situation, with given bio-
logical parents and varying levels of resources within our geographical
and social worlds. There is nothing fair or equitable about this givenness.
Some of us, for whatever reason, are born into white privilege and literate
dominance of cultural meaning. Others of us are born into radical poverty, in lands with no fresh water and very little chance of a long, healthy
life. Even others of us are born into grueling poverty amidst affluence,
working three jobs and still unable to make ends meet. Even others are
born into environments of extreme spiritual poverty, driven by cultural
forces that imprison hearts, minds, and soul in "golden handcuffs" out of
which one does not even know to struggle. Not one of us gets to choose
our own givenness; it is simply what is. The telling and hearing of our
different stories, over shared time and space, may be the only way for
incredibly diverse peoples to build relationships within and beyond that
difference.

Yet the yearning for one coherent story remains strong amidst overwhelming change. Some faith communities increasingly approach the

12. Ibid., 167.

Bible as one storyline from beginning to end.[13] There are arguable reasons to do so, of course—coherence, understanding of God's intentions within an increasingly diverse whole, clarity for storytelling, and more. But one-story approaches may miss the value of freely shared knowledge, openness to historical accuracy and scientific rigor that actually shows God's grandeur to be greater and more unimaginable than previously allowed. Walter Brueggemann speaks of this desire to form God or God's story into a conceivable-to-us form as a prose world attempting to flatten the incontrovertibly poetic.[14] The wide diversity of stories, needing to be told and needing to be heard, shows a world in dire need of transformation for the redemptive purposes of God.

CONTEMPORARY RESISTANCE

All of us will personally resist knowing our own stories and those of others in their entirety, for a variety of reasons. Historians talk despairingly about those who do not know their history. These unfortunate ones become an impoverished and even dangerous people, blindly wandering in a desert of good intentions. I see this phenomenon in pastors who, in fear of their shadows, repress their own stories from their families of origin or previous injuries. They often wind up repeating similar events in different but thematically similar congregations. I see it in faithful, theological faculty who yet treat themselves, their colleagues, and their students as they have been painfully treated in yet unclaimed narratives. I see it in congregations who are unaware of their collective story, and therefore remain in its thrall regardless of who is called as pastor. It is human to resist seeing things we do not want to see, but this resistance breeds neglect and denial, even self-ignorance.

Ignorance and neglect can also be logical, if undesired. Innumerable people have had their stories stolen from them—by slavery, by grueling poverty, by hunger, by other social injustices. Entire family lines vanished when colonialists and slave-traders ripped the domestic fabric of other cultures, other communities, leaving their descendants without an ancestrally-rooted voice for speaking today. Those brothers and sisters must find personal stories rooted in histories of choice or circumstance. They

13. See the new revised translation of the New International Version of the Bible, *The Story: Read the Bible as One Seamless Story from Beginning to End.*

14. Brueggemann, *Finally Comes the Poet*, 2.

may be too weary to claim such roots, or see their power. Others have received unfamiliar stories from dominant cultural voices that presume to tell the story of all though it be only the story of a few. Even to perceive the dominant stories as unfamiliar or inaccurate takes incredible effort of awakening, anger, grief, negotiation, liberation, and wisdom. Sometimes it's just easier to acquiesce to the dominant storyline. Women have wrestled in various ways with this understanding of dominant stories not of their own voice. In what is now a classic text, *In a Different Voice*, Carol Gilligan identified "woman's place in man's life cycle," as researched and interpreted in twentieth-century psychological-developmental theory.[15] Instead of accepting the face value of (then) current moral theory, she delved into innumerable interviews and critical research to challenge notions previously accepted within the dominant view of women's moral action. "Women's moral weakness . . . an apparent diffusion and confusion of judgment is . . . inseparable from women's moral strength, an overriding concern with relationships and responsibilities. The reluctance to judge may itself be indicative of the care and concern for others that infuse the psychology of women's development . . . "[16] Instead of accepting the dominant story-line, Gilligan labored to identify the strength of women's moral actions, rooted in "relationships and responsibilities" arguably more valued by women than by men.

Still others devalue personal stories as uncritical and unnecessary for truly rigorous thought, theological or otherwise. The task, after all, is to make oneself as objective as possible, and that means to maintain objective distance in order to observe. Personal stories are too personal to be objectively true, goes the view.

I think we also resist personal stories because it is difficult to hear, simultaneously, that we are infinitely more than we know and infinitely less than we think. A good friend from my own seminary years once quipped, "I may not be much, but I'm all I think about." Jewish wisdom offers a similar sense, if without the smiling sarcasm: "Keep two pieces of paper in your pockets at all times. One that says "I am a speck of dust." And the other, "The world was created for me."[17] We are more than we

---

15. Gilligan, *In a Different Voice*, 5–23.

16. Ibid., 16.

17. Rabbi Bunim of P'shiskha, quoted in Kula, *Yearnings*, ix.

can possibly imagine *and* we are less significant than the others around us.

For instance, some of us have been socialized into a deep self-denial valued by faithful theological traditions heavily focused upon the sinfulness of humankind. Utter depravity is hard to deny. Sin recognized and confessed paradoxically liberates human beings to move past separation into reconciliation and communion. But how dare anyone deny the very selves whom God treasures, whom God has created to be sacred, good, cherished? How dare we hide our lights under bushels, or talents in the ground? Faith demands we share what we have been given with the community in a world starved for our deepest passions.

Others of us have been affirmed in self-assertion throughout our lives, with thereby perceived potential and passionate conviction for assertive leadership. Our congregations have expressed such confidence in our gifts, our potential for speaking for others, that it is easy to think, "I am a messenger of God and will proclaim what I know to be True." But how dare we presume to speak the wholly other God, even in words of scripture, in brash conviction? Even "the least of these" is to be higher, more holy, than we are! How can we do anything but stand in silence, in the face of twentieth-century horrors inflicted on millions? How can we possibly know intimately what it is like for a suffering child to be suffering as a child, or an immigrant trying to make her way in a foreign (to her) culture, or an old man who sits in the donut shop alone in his own defenses against intimacy of any kind? Even when we have trodden a similar path? We are so much less than we think, have so little to offer. And yet infinitely more than we know.

And then awakening happens. A willingness to know the heights and depths of personal giftedness and limitation, somehow promises the knowledge of God. Greater self-knowledge leads to revelatory encounters with both self and God, only apprehended in our bones, within our being. Resistance to knowing personal stories prevents us from seeing or participating in what is most human, and ironically, most divine. When we resist, again and again, we fail to know, truly, who and whose we are. We miss the depth and breadth of knowing God.

STORYING AND BEING STORIED: SPIRITUAL
AUTOBIOGRAPHY AND CASE-STUDY RESEARCH

Two critical-contextual approaches to storied-knowing within shaping faith communities are spiritual autobiography and the sharing of case-studies or particular events within structured, shared reflection. As a paradigm of knowing, spiritual autobiography draws us into deeper self-knowledge, interrelated somehow to the knowledge of God, and revelatory of both for present purposes. It re-educates individualistic yet isolated persons in the gracious but demanding covenantal intimacy with God, made flesh today in human companions of intentional commitment. Case-studies represent a kind of social-science research aimed at a more-advanced, collaborative inquiry into self- and God-knowledge within ministry or interpersonal events-in-context. This research method structures the investigation of particular situations that evoke *how* or *why* questions but that cannot be quantified without injury to the subjects being studied. This method also builds upon the practice of spiritual autobiography in that it shows the intersection of personal narrative(s) and broader contexts of relationship, observed by an observer-participant and by covenantal companions intent upon the healthy maturation of spiritual practice toward theological wisdom.

Spiritual Autobiography

"In front of all these people you do not know, you are going to tell your life's story, particularly those details you fear most." Gasp. I could not breathe. Of course, the group leader did not actually say those words, but they are the words I heard. She probably said something more like, "The first part of our time together as a small group will be getting to know one another and ourselves a bit better. To do this, you will write a spiritual autobiography and share it with us." Spiritual autobiography? Shared with a group of people I did not know very well?! My own anxiety skyrocketed and I began to compile arguments from within my previous theological training for why such a process was unnecessary, invasive, and inappropriate. But I also had no reason then to know what I know now: facing the entirety of one's personal story within an intentional, listening community offers a daring but genuinely theological path to authentic voice, faithful witness, fearless service, and perfected wisdom.

I know now that Calvin was right—facing myself within a covenantal community led somehow to a deeper and deeper apprehension of God-knowledge, known in my bones and rooted somehow in my very spirit, by the grace of God.

This kind of story-formed community and narrative way of knowing also find great support within theological scholarship today, though the practical implications of that knowledge for lives of covenantal discipleship are harder to see clearly, to live into concrete expression.[18] As described in Chapter One, knowing *about* does not always translate into knowing *how* or a willingness to participate. The sharing of spiritual autobiographies within an intentional listening community is a combination of three "practices of faith," namely testimony, discernment, and the shaping of communities.[19] What is often overlooked is this combination of practices as an embodied and deeply participatory way of knowing, as well as doing.[20] When gently encouraged within a community of grace, however, covenantal companions unearth aspects of their own personal stories, each with the other, which then may deepen self-awareness and self-acceptance of all involved. Even the shadow-side(s) of human being becomes an unexpected strength, a source of creative energy, a place of tangible grace. Ordinary facts of event and circumstance, revealed and interpreted within a covenantal community of grace, root a human being deeply within a theological identity, to be gifted and grown into a life of faithful discipleship, courageous action, expressive delight, and spiritual integrity. This identity forms only by knowing one's own story, however, in the context of the stories of one's past, in the context of God's story given witness in historical and re-forming traditions.[21]

One manner of storied knowing comes in terms of practices that bridge theory and action, theology and beliefs, thought into discipleship.[22]

18. Hauerwas, "Story-Formed Community"; Hauerwas and Jones, *Why Narrative?*; Belenky et al., *Women's Ways of Knowing.*

19. Bass, *Practicing Our Faith*, 91–132.

20. Dykstra, "Reconceiving Practice," in *Shifting Boundaries*, 45–46.

21. See especially Morgan, *Remembering Your Story*, Peace, *Spiritual Autobiography*, and Wakefield, *Story of Your Life* for additional resourcing in biblical metaphor and personal story. Powers and Mandelker, *Pilgrim Souls*, gives classical and contemporary expressions of this storying practice.

22. MacIntyre, *After Virtue*; Bourdieu, *Outline of a Theory of Practice*; Bass, *Practicing Our Faith*; Dykstra, *Growing in Faith*; Volf and Bass, *Practicing Theology*; Bass and Richter, *Way to Live*; Bass, *Practicing Congregation.*

In popular view, Christian practice refers to "things Christian people do together over time to address fundamental human needs in response to and in the light of God's active presence for the life of the world [in Jesus Christ]."[23] An admittedly over-broad definition, but it does open doors to consider whatever we do as faithful activity *in response to the light of God's active presence*. Specific activities have historically been associated with Christian practice understood in this way: "honoring the body, hospitality, household economics, saying yes and saying no, keeping Sabbath, testimony, discernment, shaping communities, forgiveness, healing, dying well, and singing."[24] There remain important distinctions among respective authors about this list of practices—is it exclusive to Christianity? Comprehensive enough for understanding Christian discipleship? No, and no. This way of thinking is intended to broaden awareness to theology as a way of life. It is to bridge the increasing gap between intellectual analysis and lives of faith lived in the world. It therefore does not intend to inform, in a *precise* fashion, many of our more analytical questions about faith and practice, belief, and ethics. This way of thinking, of knowing, *does* bring us back repeatedly to the protracted ambiguities of our era and the necessity to meet anxiety with self-inquiry through storying, not an imposed absolutism or presumed universalism.

Spiritual autobiography therefore integrates testimony, discernment, and shaping communities into a way of knowing oneself, God, and God's covenantal community toward greater self-awareness and potentially greater self-acceptance. Scripture and tradition are chock full of testimony in various forms—narrative, but also poetry, epistles, and more—each lending particular character to God's canonical storytelling about relationship and actions with humanity in history. One could surmise that storying appears to be one of God's ways of self-revelation within history, lived experience, and communities of faith over time. Each generation of the church is faced with the challenge of hearing and telling those stories, the ones that caught the imagination of previous communities of faith, and the ones that the Spirit intends for discipleship today. Discernment is the practice that undergirds the communal awareness and claiming of those stories. Stories become real or alive when shared in communities, in the telling and the hearing, in the guidance they offer for new understand-

23. Dykstra and Bass, "A Theological Understanding of Christian Practices," in Volf and Bass, *Practicing Theology*, 18.

24. Dykstra and Bass, *Practicing Our Faith.*

ing, interpretation, wisdom. Discernment promises the active receptivity planted, tended, and harvested by communities who live alongside one another, guided by testimonies of personal, communal and divine story. Testimony offered and mutually discerned also shapes communities—in their shared identity, covenantal commitment, collaborative hopes and dreams. A community without a shared story or covenantal commitment is also being shaped, of course, but testimony and discernment structure an intentionality about a community's formation, for both good and ill. Paulo Freire observed long ago the power of naming, personal story, and active decision-making—"conscientização," in his terminology.[25]

Spiritual autobiography in this fashion portrays the gifts and growing-edges in your story, both of which will be used by the Spirit in surprising and unexpected ways. Your story shared with a healthy listening community—by which I mean one that urges you in confidence to your best self with care and challenge—offers you a glimpse of your best self, your most important gifts. Opportunity emerges to learn that the world, in one sense, was created just so gifts, like yours, could be received, offered, shared. Awareness of this opportunity entails more difficulty than you might expect, as the helping professions like ministry attract people often socialized into patterns of self-denial. Much more comfortable is the pocket paper, "I am a speck of dust." Spiritual autobiography also reminds us of this reality of human being, the limited and finite creatureliness, stewardship of which requires critical and covenantal attention to limitations and shadows. Awareness of limitation is both gift and burden, of course. It is a gift of unexpected joy to be insignificant in the face of God's glory and ultimate purposes. You are not in charge, nor can you control your community. Respecting limitations within a culture that hides finitude through professional mastery and expertise, however, requires intention and skill. Human shadows require a similar intentionality to reap what I think is their intended benefit.

Human shadows become a resource for creative, redemptive living when attended to within a listening community. Remember Peter Pan? As the story goes, Peter Pan plays tag with his shadow. He attempts to catch it, and even succeeds for brief periods of time in holding it in one place. Then he loses it once again as it plays its merry way with his desires and his attempts to control it. I personally like his playfulness with it one moment, then frustration with it the next. There is an inevitability about

25. Freire, *Pedagogy of the Oppressed*, 17.

it, as well as an honoring of fear or desire for it "not to be so." Within highly structured and morally strict communities, one's shadow may be a source of shame or guilt, but with Peter Pan's playfulness, a shadow becomes just a part of life. Ministers and theologians worth their salt not only recognize their own limitations and shadows. Through a practice of spiritual autobiography within a covenantal listening community, they can accept them with a careful playfulness as well. Not only do you receive the gift of others' awareness and support, not only are you regularly reminded of the wondrous grace and delight of a human life, in all its absurdity and potential. Spiritual autobiography unearths the potential resources available to each of us within our best selves, and within those things we attempt to hide from others.

Once you attempt to communicate the story of your life, you will realize that it is not an independent fact-collection but a process of storying out of which you cannot extricate yourself or others. You are not the list of your life's events, nor can you ever be summarized. Nonetheless, your own pursuit of wisdom requires knowing these facts, these events, facing these memories. A sustained practice of storying over time offers a deeper and deeper engagement toward wisdom within public and private exchanges—between you and you, between yourself and others, between you and God's Word. You are offered opportunities for true self-knowledge, interrelated with God through trust, reverence, and piety. This communal sharing and deep listening to personal stories then create the web of relationship that has real potential in the face of America's crisis of community. Shared personal stories weave ties of affection felt in the discovered connections and textured knots of resistance felt in hidden (or overt) disconnections with others. A communal narrative and group identity begins to form, which moves a communal story outward into broader and broader contexts of practice. A practical theological research method structures this storying outward by means of contextual analysis of a chosen event, within covenantal groups of confidentiality and carefull challenge.

Deepening the Storyline Outward: Case Studies

Practical theological scholars investigate the complex realities of God-in-community—made visible within shared understandings, practices, and interpretations—reliant upon a multitude of strategies for an even more diverse expression of interests. Some overarching themes include the interpretation of traditions through observation of congregational life, understandings of discipleship rooted in spiritual practices, moral development of persons across the human life span, and a faithful advocacy of justice within historically unjust societies.[26] Willing communities invite such research through surveys, for example, which are an increasingly common tool used by those researching congregational life and religious leadership. Any results must always be balanced with the necessary ambiguities provided in self-selecting populations who may desire to be perceived in a certain way—whether moral, proper, religious, etc.[27] Histories derived from archival resources offer another kind of glimpse into previous faith community understandings, but contemporary events for investigation may not yet have written documents. A case study is an increasingly accepted method of social science research, specifically aimed at contextual and contemporary situations with distinct characteristics.[28]

Situations that provoke *how* or *why* questions are well-suited to this kind of structured, shared reflection. Not only do case-studies offer a descriptive summary of what the researcher observes in any particular situation, they also explore the factors initially presumed and then critically assessed for contribution (or not). Secondly, case studies are useful when the investigator has little or no control over the events being studied. In contrast to biologists or psychologists who formulate hypotheses and then develop focused experiments to test those hypotheses with subject-observations, investigators of congregational life and religious leadership have little control over the events and lives they want to study. They cannot construct an experiment within a particular congregation without creating the situation they would like to examine or without doing unjust harm to well-meaning people of faith living intimate lives of discipleship in uncertain times. Increasingly, institutions of higher theological education channel all contextual research projects of students and faculty alike through an ethics discernment process, to protect congregations and those who study them for just these reasons. Within a covenantal community, however, case-study analyses deepen knowledge of self and other

26. Recent publications offer a variety of research methods into congregational life. Carroll's *God's Potters*, for instance. See also Ammerman, *Congregation and Community*.

27. Fowler, *Survey Research Methods*, 25–28, 61ff.

28. Yin, *Case-Study Research*, 15–17.

within the broader purposes of God, mutually discerned and tested over time. This approach to deeper understanding, belonging and interpretation toward wisdom suggests a most appropriate method for focusing continual learning within real-life situations.

To be clear, these terms—understanding, interpretation, and wisdom—have a long disciplinary history worth attention for many, if not all.[29] In these pages, *understanding* will refer to the personal awareness of a self-in-situation, both intuited and critically articulate within one's primary communities of discourse. *Interpretation* originates from within such a personal-communal narrative, but entails a rigorous, collaborative process that may unearth subconsciously held understandings and challenge consciously-held convictions. In the now classical work of David Kelsey, critical interpretation requires a sensitive awareness and deepening of the pre-texts in which one has developed understanding, engaged side by side with the texts and contexts of the present situation.[30] *Wisdom*—a received, impermanent, but vibrant integration of understanding and interpretation lived into a compassionate and life-affirming, embodied form—then lives its theological intensity and inspiration directed outward into the world. Cynthia Bourgeault's sense of wisdom[31] explored earlier brings new life to the often cognitively-captive nuances. Others attentive to faith formation reliant upon storying and highly oral elements of communication speak of wisdom beyond cognitive bounds into living communal forms as well.[32] Wisdom has even been called, with creative verve and in the voice of fictional character Maria Magdalena Theotoky, "the second paradise of the world."[33]

Case studies promise a method sensitive to its complexity and tenacious for what may be learned toward more faithful action. This requires a careful observation or awareness of an implicitly emotional or spiritual event, complemented by an intimate knowledge of self-in-context and a willingness to be shaped by broader contexts. A compassionate, challenging community—one that listens prayerfully for things expected and unexpected—serves as the relational web of knowing. Relationships are

---

29. Browning, *Fundamental Practical Theology*, 38ff.

30. Kelsey, *Uses of Scripture in Recent Theology*, ix.

31. Bourgeault, *Wisdom Way of Knowing*.

32. Wimberly and Parker, *In Search of Wisdom*, 23–73.

33. Davies, *Rebel Angels*, 39.

sustained only within group conversations that are intentionally covenantal, confidential, and carefully challenging. Some observations for
identification of a ministry event will clarify how to begin and then the
structured conversation that constitutes the method within covenantal
listening groups will be briefly summarized.

More advanced storied-knowing originates with the identification
of an event with some implicit or explicit energy within it. Not surprising for a relationally integrative discipline such as formation, the origin
of critical case study work requires a personal sensitivity to some event
that has snagged your unconscious or subconscious such that you have
something deeply personal to gain and yet something that is also overtly
professional in importance. I remember some powerful and unnerving
encounters I have had with Hospice patients and those facing their own
frailty in unexpected illness. These kinds of events, easily recognizable by
an overwhelm of emotion (positive or negative) or some cognitive dissonance, beg for further examination within a shared context of inquiry.
Other encounters elicit less obvious material for a case-study, though the
process can be just as valuable for the primarily relational formation and
self- and God-knowledge to come.

One easily identified encounter in my own story was with a fellow I
will call Q. I only visited him four times yet he has since been an implicit
and loving companion in my ability to listen to older men and those facing
their own deaths. He was an alcoholic who had been dry for over twenty
years, a lifelong Catholic who had little patience for religious authority,
and a deeply perceptive man who recognized my voice on the phone the
first time I called to set up a time to visit. Apparently, I had met him two
years previously, once, in a hospital room. He *knew* my voice! My visits
with him were explicitly to offer him and his family hospice care during
this time of dying, but never had I been confronted with the intensity and
variety of lessons to be learned for greater self-awareness, acceptance,
and professional ministry practice: the startling first contact; the intensity
of conversation and the immediate resonance between two people who
are not supposed to know each other very well but recognize something
deeply alive between them. Not every ministry encounter has as obvious
of material for deeply emotional awareness, startling synchronicity or
providence, or pastoral caregiving between children of God.

The less obvious events usually snag something within the subconscious, just below the surface of memory and awareness. We can begin to

identify them with various associations, such as a person simply coming to mind several times and in unexpected ways. Dreams often bring a person or an encounter with someone to our awareness and from which we would learn in case-study examinations. Other clues such as bodily weariness or cyclical thinking can alert the attentive practitioner to a ministry event that has something to teach, when examined critically through a written discipline of description, evaluation, analysis, theological reflection and communal discernment for sensitive action.[34] Identification of a ministry event then leads into a well-structured conversation for critical-contextual analysis.

Structured Conversation: Five Major Moments

This method moves through five major "moments" of description, evaluation, analysis, theological reflection, and discernment of action. A summary glimpse of the conversation here will help flesh out what kinds of things may be expected with this kind of advanced storied-knowing. Description of the identified ministry event traditionally includes brief logistical and narrative details of the encounter being investigated. If the event is a conversation, what was its basic setting? Where did it happen and with whom? What was the physical environment like? Was there anyone else around or *indirectly* involved? A verbatim conversation, written down as close to human memory as possible, gives a clear rendition of the observer's view of the event. Details like gender, age, and racial-ethnic identities are crucial, though they should be veiled in some fashion to protect the dignity and personhood of all. It will become quite apparent that you do not remember as much as you would like, nor will you be writing the conversation down as it happened. This is okay. Better, actually. The event *in your awareness* instigates the critical reflection to come.

The second moment in this method of research deepens your own awareness with intentional evaluation. The description aims for as raw of remembered data as possible. Evaluation moves this verbatim dialogue with description into a broader personal imagining or insight into what

---

34. A case-study closely resembles what Kenneth Pohly calls a "ministry reflection report." This entire method of the critical interpretation of situations parallels his process of supervision, though with intentional avoidance of the unavoidably hierarchical implications within that term. See Pohly, *Transforming the Rough Places*, 115–17.

else might have been going on, given a little critical reflection. What does the description itself suggest were the core issues at play? Not what is already known, or immediately assumed, but one-step removed? This is a challenge of letting go of your preconceived ideas and assured convictions about who this person was, what the conversation meant, how you were misunderstood or wronged, or what you did well as a minister of God. This is an invitation for you to analyze the text and verbatim conversation you have written, critically, and examine it as you would someone else's writing. Given just this text, without any body-experience of the event, what do you perceive to be the core issues at play? What is your own systemic role in the conversation? What critical question do you have about the interaction? Questions like these are asked and answered in a brief fashion.

Analysis names the third moment of the case-study conversation, though this term often refers to the whole manner of investigation being engaged here. Analysis names the step in which you deepen your understanding with texts and contexts for interpretation. What texts may encourage your own awareness? What other authors have written on topics or issues that seem to present within the ministry event? What alternative possibilities emerge for what happened? What rationales or interpretations have you avoided or discarded that could still be in play? This stage of the conversation is where your group members and possible facilitator begin to contribute perspective, but your own exploration of it before any shared conversation is an important step in pushing your own thinking, yourself.

The fourth moment brings implicit questions of God's presence and agency into the forefront. Where might God be acting or leading in the conversation, interaction, or event? How may God have been moving in your own thoughts and actions, and in those of the others involved in the interaction? Without careful monitoring, this moment can consume the focus of a theologically curious or implicitly anxious observer-participant, distracted thereby from learning crucial things about the self or the systems in which we serve. Faithful seekers and religious leaders alike often want to jump right to the theological naming step, before or during the description, definitely before the evaluation and analysis. We are about being people of God, and our task is to proclaim God to the world, after all. Yet theological reflection must remain fourth in the process for many reasons.

First, many of us are prone to name the most comforting or emotional events in our lives "acts of God." Well they may be. But more often than not, acts of God are those that startle us out of a limited understanding of who God is and what God actually desires toward the beloved community in that particular situation. Description, evaluation, and analysis—before naming what is of God or what is not of God—allows us to hear the edgy demands of scripture, of the Spirit, of a love that costs more than cheap grace. If what we perceive to be acts of God actually are, then they will withstand the challenge of critical thought. If they are not, we are commanded to discern the spirits (1 John 4:1) and so therefore must allow the possibility for reflection apart from our previous experiences and understandings of God.

Second, God's word let loose within the acts of shared ministry brings a humility of awareness and human interdependence that observable knowledge, already known, hides. If we name God's intentions without any outside, objective process, not only do we miss hearing the beautiful complexity which will undeniably be closer to what God intends, but we also miss that our knowledge is a fundamentally interrelational thing. Jean-Luc Marion qualifies knowledge, at least the knowledge for the love of wisdom, in just such a fashion: you cannot actually know something or someone you do not love. All philosophy "must begin by loving before claiming to know."[35] No matter what energies are stirred up in the ministry event you identify, you can be sure that God loves any protagonist and antagonist equally fiercely. If you felt wronged in some interaction, God's redemption of it will happen in movements toward reconciliation. If you felt you were successful in your event, God's use of it will unearth ways you could have been more sensitive or done some things differently. God's living Word will never be captivated by our own understandings, and this reality is repeatedly learned and taught when theological discernment follows a process of critical reflection begun in description, and then evaluated and analyzed before any naming begins. The gift of theological reflection, in this fourth-moment, is both clarity of perspective *and* a humility that connects the knowledge to self, God, and others.

The final moment in the case-study process is a shared discernment of overarching questions toward future action and learning to come.

---

35. Marion, *The Erotic Phenomenon*, 2.

Given a more complete picture of the encounter, what shall be done is discerned within a description that shows intended and unintended facets of the event, and in the evaluation and analysis of what has been learned, for what God may invite. If there is no discerned responsiveness, then what is the point of the learning? Cognitive understanding is one thing, but risked discipleship requires more than simply knowing more or conceiving a right interpretation. Discipleship requires a response in faith to what the Spirit has offered for relational formation, integration. It makes a claim on your life that you may not have chosen within intention but that you cannot now deny. Conviction and energy to accomplish these next steps graciously emerges within rightly chosen, discerned responses. Not always, of course, but often.

Ultimately, stories within a spiritual autobiography and those that take shape in conversation with particular contexts offer a deeply steeped and traditional way of knowing self and God in the unexpected and mundane events discerned within covenantal communities. It broadens the shared experiences of storying into a much broader web of relationships—denominationally, communally, geographically—that also has great impact on present ministry practice. Telling and listening to stories requires increased awareness and persistent practice for healthy self-acceptance and covenantal belonging with others who are just as fragile as we are. This fragility means that covenantal small groups offer promise, but also risk: risk of undesired self-knowledge, risk of over-vulnerability to others' fears and desires, risk of nurture that does not exist readily in broader society, even church and faith communities.

COVENANTAL GROUPS—LIGHT AND SHADOW

It is the pedagogical unpredictability that offers the greatest potential for a theological wisdom discovered and uncovered with those who are willing to risk, to trust, to encounter the other in themselves, together. Ministry lived close to the Holy cannot be predicted, and covenantal group learning trains expectations and observations accordingly. Unmerited grace may be received in the observation from a person who affirms, and thereby diffuses some hidden fear. Laughter and tears flow both directions around the circle. Covenantal groups can even foster boredom, if members resist the vulnerability for actual connection. Those in this process will encounter pain or injury, intended or not. Small groups of covenant form resilience and facilitate reconciliation, where possible. Such covenantal groups also create the framework of sustained relationship in which presuppositions and personal stories are gently examined. By gently, I mean *within* relationship—not as some detached object under a microscope, not a blind acceptance of some other authority—but within the web of human being where intimate realizations are not analyzed but stretched to include more than "our own." It is this web of relationship, so often dissected within traditional classroom pedagogies, that enlivens theology as an historical argument, a proposition needing new breath and disagreement, a way of life for people who hunger and thirst.

My first entrance into safely structured peer-group learning was excruciating because I had always avoided small group settings—whether cliques in high school, sports teams, or even Bible studies that felt "too close." For most of the informal times when some small group activity was proposed, I would be sure to have a book to read or an errand to run. I kept a safe distance that way. I also failed to derive any benefits from shared lives, however. Imagine my surprise when I entered a facilitated peer-group—intended for safe-space, interpersonal process, and theological reflection—that completely challenged my own perceptions and assumptions. I did not know the members of this group, nor had I chosen them. To be fair, they had not chosen me either. We were placed into a peer-group process in which we were to interact with one another, and learn how to do so for both personal gains in identity and self-awareness, and for interpersonal skill development.

Any boot camp has its own culture of unchosen but instant-intimacy, and this group was no different in that respect. The smells of our working environment were sometimes overwhelming and even offensive. The emotional tasks of listening, presence, prayer were tiring with few obvious results for our efforts. Writing tasks were assigned, in addition to the long hours of visitation and class time, and those tasks presented integrative challenges of intimacy *and* textual finesse. The small group became both haven and havoc for interpersonal wisdom of some importance for my desire to serve God and others. As my new colleagues-in-ministry risked sharing parts of themselves that contemporary culture usually hides, I learned the rare beauty of human fragility and vulnerable courage. As I dared to explore the hidden parts of my own story, my own way of being in the world, I received a confirmation and acceptance I had never experienced before. All of these elements, within the supervised and carefully tended environment of a peer-group, unearthed what I had conceived as "theological education" and put in its place a wildly untidy but intimately authentic process of formation. I now understand the value of a good, healthy covenantal group.

Not all small group experiences are life-transformative, however. People who disavow and critique peer-group learning do so with justification and righteous affront. Small groups can damage a person's sense of safety, ability to trust, confidence in oneself. Even well-facilitated groups may take on a dangerous life of their own, which the trained facilitator can only tend, or direct, not prevent. The best and the worst of the human condition enters into the forming group's process, and members are forced to respond and learn from both. Particular practices of covenant, confidentiality, and challenge can maximize the gifts of covenantal groups while minimizing the difficulties, which are yet part of the gift.

Covenant, Confidentiality, Challenge

Covenantal commitment, each group member to the other and if possible, a facilitator to each group member, establishes the space in which deepening engagement and even intimacy can develop. Whether initially conscious of it or not, each member of a covenant group eventually faces a moment of decision about depth of participation, the extent of vulnerability and the potential gifts to be received. How much risk can be borne? For what do they hope as the companionship deepens? When discomfort or even outright anger arises, what does the rhythm of self-assertion and self-surrender in God's covenantal love require? Of course, this is not love in the modern notion, a sentimental humanity, or wisps of romantic nostalgia between two soulmates. It is a willingness of diverse human beings to enter into something larger than human persons, something or Someone who will create humanity anew, even as finite frailty remains. Each covenantal companion is still responsible for speaking what the other group members cannot mind-read. You are still responsible for your share of the group process, maintenance, and ingenuity for serving, loving, engaging the other. It is the willingness that changes you, and potentially grows that change into the group and then beyond into the world.

It is this covenant of steadfast love, noted in Jewish and Christian scriptures with *hesed* and resonant with the non-theistic, Tibetan Buddhist notion of *samaya*,[36] that runs through the entire journey of God's people. It is a journey that courses through the rivers and mountains of healthy sustainable living, living into the world in new ways through all those who are so willing. This speaks an authentic humanity, gracious steward-ship and perfect wisdom. The commitment changes a person, potentially more. It makes each of you more of who you are to become, even as it does not wipe out individuality or character. Be forewarned: covenantal commitment does not make you happy or fulfilled. Each group member must hold onto herself, in the deep resonances that happen with some group members, and in the uncomfortable mirroring that both difference and identification can offer. But when a group embraces such a covenant, over a longer period of time and through thick and thin, the web of re-lationships can light a fire deep within that is unquenchable and satisfies yearning, but for the grace of the sacred that draws us ever onward.

What all this means practically is that as a group member, your responsibility is to listen deeply to all aspects of the interaction—the presentation, participatory reading, other group members' engagement, broader context or environment—with a persistent prayer for and deep-ening awareness of the presenter's health, awareness, and growth. How might you live into God's form for that person? What is your way, in speech or in silence, to embody God's primary grace and merciful justice in the here and now of the group's interaction? You live out your own covenantal commitment within God's intentions and within the unpre-dictable process of group interaction when you listen for how you are to serve the other, share your felt-senses, mirror what you see, and inquire further into the unfolding conversation.

Confidentiality is the second area of skill development for any small group work, living out their covenant with one another. The word means different things in different environments, but for peer-groups, it means "what happens in group, stays in the group." Doctors are to honor the confidentiality of their patient-doctor relationship. Observe the at-tempts to control information about who is in the hospital and who is not. Lawyers maintain client-attorney privilege, though they also know particular instances when privileged information can be forced out in court. Few lawyers keep private journals, for instance, knowing that they can become permissible evidence in courts of law. Seasoned pastoral

---

36. Rig'dzin Dorje, *Dangerous Friend*, 105.

ministers also know that church communities have a near-instant infor-
mational network of neighbors, whether true friends or historical an-
tagonist-enemies. Confidentiality within the pastorate is one of the most
complex and difficult skills to learn. Peer-groups who covenant to keep
their process confidential begin to learn the necessary skills for communication with sensitivity to collegial and congregational confidentiality.
Perhaps this seems overwhelmingly improbable or unlikely, particularly
in congregational settings. Think of it this way: the rigor of confidentiality practiced will prefigure the level of trust in the group: less trust, then
less risk, less intimacy, and ultimately, less growth in the interpersonal
engagement with one another. The group decides, in the end, not even
the leader of the group.

Practices of confidentiality in this process are also part of a service to
the other and to the communities beyond the contexts of the group itself.
Any written documents—spiritual autobiographies, case-studies, theological statements of any kind—are to be handled with the utmost care,
which means received for the time they are to aid the group's interaction,
and then returned to the original author in order to honor the sanctity
of interpersonal process and human dignity. Inevitably, the temptation to
figure out the precise persons, places, and events of peoples' stories arises.
Confidentiality requires that this temptation be identified, recognized in
some fashion within yourself, and let go or pursued no further in awareness or speech. This is a mental discipline that increases with practice, like
most things. If the presenter unintentionally neglects practices of confidentiality within his or her written documents, then a gentle reminder of
the importance of confidentiality becomes your responsibility as well.

Another crucial yet difficult skill to learn I call "care-full challenge."
Peer-groups offer one of the few opportunities in the life of faith to actually receive honest feedback about one's own story, behavior, or unseen
quirks. The safety of the group environment must be paramount for everyone to feel an invitation to risk or become a little more vulnerable
to others' sight. Gentle truth-telling within such a group can then offer
its members an advantage of perspective largely unavailable outside its
bounds. Most environments exact either relational or professional cost
for frailty, mistakes, vulnerability. Vulnerability in a deeply intimate relationship may offer healthy intimacy for both partners, but it will not
be easy, nor will it necessarily *feel* good. Unhealthy vulnerability in the
workplace can be deadly, for both professional performance of tasks and

collegial comfort. Yet healthily risked vulnerability gives a wealth of insight, when done with great care in a peer-group designed for just that purpose.

Challenge with care, as a shared group practice, is easiest to describe as either a boomerang or a rubber band. Anything, I mean *anything* that you observe or perceive to be "a gentle challenge" for the presenter in the interactions of the group's process is first to be assessed *for what it has to teach you.* There may be something of importance that Spirit wants you to share with the speaker or with another group member, but it would not have arisen within your own awareness if it did not have something to do with your own story, your own desires, your own needs. This is the boomerang effect of group process. Many of us have not been trained to throw a boomerang correctly, but it is still possible to throw one *without* care. We throw it with great zeal and confidence. It does not come back precisely to us, but hits trees, other people, or objects in the vicinity. Similarly, whatever we throw away from us with some force, without the careful skills of self-monitoring, will unintentionally create pain and potential injury. Our own fears, needs, and desires may hit those who happen to be in our vicinity, such as other group members. Rubber-bands held with tension between two people require the same care. If one loses hold on what the "challenge for the other" has to do with his experience, then the rubber band will snap with potentially painful force against the hands, mind, faith, or even body of the other person holding the rubber band. Care-full challenge, on the other hand, is connectional, relational, constructive, if both participants—all group members—watch for new awareness within themselves first, then awareness to be directed outward into the group.

Remember, our families of origin predispose us—before we ever enter into group conversations—to trusting our environment with a sense of curiosity or fearing it with a sense of deep mistrust. Previous settings of context condition expectations about present and future contexts, not in a predestined way, but in a way that honors all those things that came before, that frame how we observe events, how we engage others, and how we may open (or not) to the good, the true, the beautiful gifts of human community. Erik Erikson spells this out in his logic of human development beginning with elemental trust in safe family environments and primal distrust in those that threaten the physical or emotional well-being of persons—from earliest infancy well into the human life-span.[37] Others portray the human capacity to reach outside ourselves, funded by desires or a sense of something or Someone greater than ourselves, which then may be welcomed or just as easily shut out or defended against. Some theologians such as Wolfhart Pannenberg have called this "exo-centricity,"[38] while others simply name it "spirit," or the unwelcome guest in any knowing event.[39] Contemplative psychologist Gerald May assures that this human force for life cannot be ignored forever, though many of us try with apathy, addictions, and more. Regardless, May observes, "there are times each day when we are forced to wake up to the fact of being alive; times when conscious choices must be made about what to do or how to be."[40] Dorothy Holland and her team refer to this phenomenon as the unavoidable self-authoring of identity in cultures.[41] Our immediate families of origin condition our abilities to act or defer action, to perceive wonder and threat, regardless of individual propensity for either. Well-defended or careful participation in this group practice of challenge is not a moral failing but a behavior for observation, care, and sensitive invitations beyond.

In sum, healthy small groups who organize their ongoing *communitas* or *koinonia* with these practices promise a truly counter-cultural path for deepening self- and other-awareness, building (or straining) peer-relationships, ultimately observing one's received or embedded theology in action within the context(s) served. The temptation to exact these behaviors in terms of a binding contract or mutual agreement within the framework of law increases in today's over-legalized regulation of human relationships, for good and ill.

CONCLUSION

Theologian Miroslav Volf draws a fitting and distinctive conclusion for covenantal companionship amidst these practices of covenant, confidentiality, and care-full challenge. In a continuum of contract and covenant

---

37. Erikson, *Identity and the Life Cycle*, 57–67.
38. Pannenberg, *Anthropology in Theological Perspective*, 37ff.
39. Loder, *Transforming Moment*, 2.
40. May, *Will and Spirit*, 5.
41. Holland et al., *Identity and Agency in Culture*, 169–91.

and embrace, he notes that a covenant and a contract are quite different,[42] in terms of expectations, durability and governance. Volf observes that covenants are unconditional and contracts are conditional. In contracts, we are obliged to keep the terms only if our partners are doing the same. One can feel the *quid pro quo* character within a contract. In contrast, covenants are unconditional, determined by God's promises to us, not our own to each other or to God. A small group covenant, rooted in God's love and justice combined, subverts the wisdom of the world with a divine, deeply relational logic. Injury is not to be met with injury, but with truth, justice, peace shared in compassion amidst others' oversight.

Second, contracts are temporary: we are bound by them only as long as it suits us and our interests. This one is harder to identify in contexts of teaching/learning that are sustained by theological institutions for just a short time, but covenants within groups are durable beyond individual preference and pattern. The context of one's group holds us in its crux or crucible where we stay when we want to and when we would rather leave. The group covenants together to withstand and celebrate all aspects of human frailty, in order to witness to the larger context in which divine endurance sustains interdependence and covenantal relationship. Covenantal groups are durable, together. Finally, Volf reminds us that covenants, not contracts, are governed by the demands of love, compassion, and just mercy. Contracts are useful, legally binding, pragmatic relationships in which participation is governed by the pursuit of one's interests. Covenantal commitment within your group speaks to a deepening discipleship within practices of love, service, compassion, and justice for all, within and beyond the group—aspects of which may be personally demanding or even threatening to one's previous self-image and understanding of call.

All group members, whether presenting or listening, must develop presence, intention, and awareness for the explicit, implicit, and null aspects of the unfolding conversation. The processes described and the objectives listed in chapter 1 name the explicit curriculum intended by formation as interpreted here. Yet the implicit curriculum of this process has its own gifts to be received, if intentionally pursued. What is the body language of the presenter and those participating (or less so) in the group process? Were there any slips-of-the-tongue—by which I

42. Volf, *Exclusion and Embrace*, 147ff.

mean unintended words spoken in the dialogue but not written in the text—in the participatory reading of a document? Those *may* signal something in the subconscious that could become conscious with more scrutiny. They may not, however. How anxious is the group, as a whole, and what are some of the potential causes of that anxiety? What is the overall level of engagement or presence within the group's members? People have different strategies for coping with uncomfortable aspects of the group process—felt vulnerability, anger, frustration, desire, sadness, or fear—and these strategies are often integral to the implicit curriculum of the group. For myself, for both good and ill, I will often multi-task or make lists in groups or meetings during which I perceive high anxieties or disrespect of persons or process and during which I have little ability to direct or control group outcomes. Sometimes that is healthy for me and the group, other times it is not. Finally, it is important to be reminded regularly that not everything *means* something, or at least means something to be shared *aloud*. Determining meaning for every jot and tittle of a group's process can strangle the spontaneity of the group and the enjoyment shared between members just living their lives and exploring their gifts. Sometimes life is just to be lived, not analyzed, interpreted, and articulated to death.

A willingness to learn one's own story and allow it to be woven into a broader communal story signals not the self-centered obsessions of a popularizing Americana, but a motivating humility and potentially re-demptive vulnerability for radically covenantal community. Instead of personal stories for the sake of self-expression, such stories open our eyes to gifts we never knew we had, and growing edges we were most fearful to acknowledge. What we do with those gifts and edges remains to be seen, engaged, with intention or without it. Authentically covenantal commu-nities—those who intentionally practice covenant, confidentiality, and care-full challenge together over time—begin to live a communal story that many of us in rooted theological traditions recognize within our extensive historical, theological, and scriptural witnesses. Relationships are somehow sustained through disagreement and mutual transforma-tion until lived awareness of human interdependence grows, glimpsed again and again. Loneliness evaporates amidst a connective solitude and compassionate delight in human complexities.

These covenantal companionships *are* becoming more and more prevalent, as more established institutions face overwhelming change and uncertain identities within new cultural currents. Consider ancient-future groups of religious belonging sometimes called *emergent,* or so-called megachurches, whose communal life thrives because of massive small group ministries. Consider spiritual companionships in terms of spiritual direction, coaching, holy friendship, covenant groups. This companionship is less theologically or ideologically identifiable because the purpose is a deepening spiritual intimacy, a radically covenantal discipleship lived in spiritual practice and risked mission.

Even covenantal companionships require a broader context and shared story, however, if they are to remain life-affirming and continuously restorative of companionable delight shared alongside sufferings of self and others. Once lonely or spiritually hungry persons find a resource in each other to nourish their deepest hungers, temptations will arise to hoard, to protect oneself from any diffusion or loss of newly received intimacies. But like manna in the wilderness, these gifts of covenantal community cannot be stored for individual gain or protection. They are only truly received when given outward, into broader contexts and other stories. Additionally, any growing human community will necessarily face issues of its organization—communication, collective support, leadership, practices. Linked, radically covenantal communities are no different, in that respect.

Classical theology here offers a Story of God in innumerable voices toward nourishing an intimacy that needs to be shared in order to be received. With wisdom resources from communities of God over the centuries, theology offers entrance into this Story to encourage communities to face natural growing pangs of communal life. This Story is infinitely more complex than anyone can conceive or articulate, but remember, the task is not necessarily to know all the right details. The task is to awaken and become a participant in a story larger than your own, made available to you within your own stories shared outward, such that smaller communities may live together into God's rhythms, grace, and transformations. Established institutions of theological education offer an overflowing treasure-store of resources for this task, even as one needs to be attentive to growing self-awareness and one's particular gifts and voice within covenantal companionship.

4

Shaped By God's Story:
Becoming a Seasoned Apprentice-Artisan

This chapter brings the storied way of knowing into the realm of words about God, guided by the purposes of God into both historically-conscious and contextual expressions, intertwined each with the other. The humility and vulnerability that undergird a storying way of knowing are counter-cultural, however, at least within many of today's established institutions of theological education. There one finds a virtual treasure-trove of resources and, often, institutional demands antagonistic for intuitive knowing, deeper spiritual practice, and valued communal wisdom. Most of us who enter into formal learning programs within higher education have been schooled to think of education as an information-transmission, content-achievement process toward mastery of subject.[1] Learning in this sense is less about the self and more about the subject. Established institutions of theological education must navigate this schooling culture, as entering students are required to become versed in their own theological traditions, for which they will become primary tradition-bearers. Habits of mind in these instances require an immediate cognitive split between content and person, information and process. The manner of knowing that unknows for the sake of a deeper covenant and mutual transformation challenges this schooling model of education or formally programmatic learning. This dissonance is difficult to sustain, though made easier within primarily relational communities of covenant.

Thankfully, there are as many entrances into God's Story as there are the proverbial rooms within God's mansions. The draw of deeper spiritual practice represents a discovered hallway. The potential resting places

---

1. Gardner, *Unschooled Mind*, 126–42. See also Palmer, *To Know as We are Known*, 33ff.

in such a pursuit of theological wisdom are innumerable. The school-ing-storying tension, however, plays out here in the hallway between an *objective, well-defined approach* to God's Story refined by historical consciousness and a *lived, refining theology-in-context* approach to God's Story, lived into complex expressions that are traditional yet intimately particular. Both approaches offer their gifts for continually new and traditionally-rooted voices. The next step in this process of intentional formation, then, is to find one's own voice, grounded in personal story and shared outward into covenantal community for a shared life in God, for the other, in the world. Delight will be found here, with enough time and tenacity of spirit.

THEOLOGY WITH MANY ROOMS

Most of theology's senses are legitimate within their own contexts, though human persons wax and wane with which one serves God most faithfully. "Which is right, or most coherent or systematic or construc-tive etc.?" may not be the most helpful questions, though they offer truth in their rigor. Innumerable writers with classically established perspec-tive consider theology to be words about God, etymologically defensible with *logos* and *theos* as roots: word, God. A dialectical tension emerges between a contemplative approach—unitive experience of God, union with God—and a cognitive or analytical approach—thinking about God—which presupposes the conceptual remove of a self thinking about God. The former suggests an eradication of the self into union. The latter requires a differentiation that erases union within the subjective/objec-tive split of consciousness.[2] An earliest sense of theology within Christian traditions refers to "an actual, individual cognition of God and things re-lated to God."[3] It companions faith and aims for eternal happiness, being delightedly found in the Presence. Theology here is both a *habitus* and a *scientia,* or a habit of the soul in which the true is distinguished from the false.[4] Another referent for theology is as a discipline, "a self-conscious scholarly enterprise of understanding."[5] This brought with it educational or pedagogical associations, often described with the word *dialectic.* Ed-

2. May, *Will and Spirit,* 44ff.
3. Farley, *Theologia,* 31.
4. Ibid., 32.
5. Ibid., 31.

ward Farley traces these distinctions through three historical eras aiming for understandings of *theology/scientia* or *knowledge* and *theology/discipline* over the course of nearly two thousand years.[6] One could say a lot about the meaning of "theology" over the years.

Architecture of Theology

One classically disciplined view of theology comes from a well-respected theologian with systematic impulses. Alister McGrath structures theology's plot and functions into six major areas, with disciplinary specialization in mind.[7] It is foolish to attempt a summary of these things, but just to give you a start, I will be a little foolish.

McGrath introduces disciplinary theology with Etienne Gilson's image of the great systems of scholastic theology as the "cathedrals of the mind."[8] True to Christian theology's historical development with an ever-present eye on the Bible, McGrath begins with *biblical studies*. This room stores resources and offers breathing space for those scholars and guild-organizations intent upon the exegetical or critical biblical foundations for theological understanding. Biblical studies folks include all kinds of specialists in ancient languages, original manuscripts, archaeology, histories of interpretation, and more. The important point is primary attention to the interpretation and understanding of biblical texts for theological understanding amidst contemporary challenges of knowledge, faith, and community. Because of contemporary challenges to theological disciplines and the centrality of the question of scriptural authority today, you often find biblical departments to be the strongest political centers of theological education institutions. Not always, but it is often the case, particularly in seminaries that maintain close connections with local congregations and denominations focused upon issues of authority.

Systematic theology describes an approach to theological understanding organized by educational or presentational concerns, or on presuppositions about method. Systematics engages theological understanding with particular attention to historically argued theologies, their doctrinal interrelationships, and rigor or invalidity of previous doctrines for speak-

6. Ibid., 33ff.

7. McGrath, *Christian Theology*, 141–48.

8. Ibid., 141.

ing about God and God's work in the world today. Systematics involves a wide variety of disciplinary voices, from foci in ethics and constructive theology to interdisciplinary integrations of history and scripture study.

Historical theology describes an approach to theological understanding intent upon the interconnections between theological ideas or doctrines and the historical situations within which these ideas developed. A distinct but related guild network shows historical theology to refer to those who teach church history within theological education, but also those who have scholarly interests in historical scriptural or theological interpretation—how Genesis was interpreted in commentaries by ancient church fathers or how mystical theology actually roots in the contemplative lives of ancient to medieval women, for instance.

Practical theology approaches theological understanding with a similar focus upon context, but offers its description, evaluation, normativity, and proscription with sensitivity to historical precursors *and* contemporary demands or challenges. This kind of theology, sometimes aligned with pastoral theology, engages theological understanding with particular interest in contemporary models of transformative action. More precisely, though, pastoral theology is an entire discipline unto itself, with roots in psychology, human development, clinical pastoral education, and classical theological disciplines. Sometimes it can include poetry, in one scholar I know. Practical theology also describes, or becomes described by, separate disciplines engaged by preachers (called homileticians, informed by scriptural exegesis, public speaking, and rhetoric), liturgical theologians or worship scholars (including church musicians), congregational analysts (often called congregational studies researchers), and educators trained in historical and contemporary integrations of education, psychology, philosophy, and faith practice. These separate disciplinary scholars do not all self-identity as practical theologians, however. Never will you find one designation like practical theology chosen by all across this multitude of disciplinary specializations, though they may all be assessed by others as practical theologians, against their collective will.

Philosophical theology enters into the theological enterprise with a special commitment to questions of human existence, regardless of tradition or historical perspective. This lens in the architecture of theology allows questions to be asked independent of method, and then answered from a variety of historical and contemporary angles, grounded in a common dialogue about shared human experience. The early marriage of Christian communities and classical Greek philosophy within which to articulate these communities' self-understandings insured that a sometimes uncomfortable but historically unavoidable dialogue—multilogue, actually—was born and continued into contemporary wrestling with human existence in a non-faith identified philosophy and systematic or historical theology.

Finally, *spirituality* and *mystical theology* address theological understanding from the direct interior knowledge of God, experience of God and the transformation of lives. "Christian spirituality" names the discipline relatively recently established and recognized within the American Academy of Religion. It is carefully qualified, in contrast to this brief summary, but it aims at a general material object of study: spirituality as an existential phenomenon, related to human persons across cultural and conceptual categories.[9] Mystical theology is often differentiated from Christian spirituality, but both lenses within McGrath's architecture of theology identify the inescapably intimate and categorically human phenomenon of mystical knowledge of God, beyond analytical precision but not outside of articulate accuracy for theological understanding. Both are only rigorously constituted, however, within the lives of concrete, believing subjects critically examined and creatively interpreted toward a faithful integration into lived discipleship today.

The world of the academy is built upon a myriad of important distinctions in the above paragraphs, distinctions that I am avoiding for the sake of our storied way of knowing here and its primacy for encouraging intentional formation within immediate covenantal communities of faith. The distinctions are not unimportant, but they have the most to contribute within a different frame of knowing, less overtly connected to personal stories and context. It is spectacular to explore the distinctions, but not necessarily part of a deepening discipleship for early theological study or a peripheral community's risked missions. Other authors within and outside of disciplinary purview have introductory approaches too, one of which is worth particular mention.

Theological ethicist Christopher Morse engages the tasks of theological understanding and articulation from an intuitive and unexpected angle: disbelief. The governing principle here is that in order to believe

---

9. Schneiders, "Approaches to the Study of Christian Spirituality," 15–33.

something, to truly put one's weight on presuppositions and convictions you will hold as they change within a life of Christian ministry, you also have things that you cannot believe. Morse writes, "the truth in Christian doctrine harbors a lie whenever the faithful disbeliefs these doctrines entail go unrecognized. . . . There are some things that Christian faith refuses to believe." [10] I find this refreshing and illuminating within populations who focus solely on articulating their beliefs, when lives and actions suggest disbelief at some level as well. Morse's work arises in an intersection between systematic theology and practical theology, though in disciplinary terms, his view comes from a subset of systematics, Christian ethics. His method begins with a scriptural imperative to test the spirits of the age (1 John 4:1). Articulate theologies must be tested over time for validity, from various angles, each of which conveniently begins with the letter "C": coherence, cruciality, consequence, conformity with conscience, consonance with experience, catholicity, consistency with worship, congruence with scripture, continuity with Apostolic Tradition, and comprehensiveness. [11] The best way to determine theological validity with sensitivity to the gospel given witness in scripture, tradition, reason, and experience is to test its rigor by means of these established criteria which regularly, together, discern the actions of God within one's life, church, world. For an articulate theology, this kind of approach offers you a flexible signpost to assess your own thinking. How will your theological reflection demonstrate this careful attention and loving participation in past wisdom, present experience, and future invitation?

Practical Theology: A Storied Way with Architectural Pillars

A disciplinary perspective that offers both received rigor and supple strength for crafting a theological perspective can be named *theology-in-context*, though the more creative, lively image for this perspective has already been introduced as an *artisanal theology*. Consider an event I attended where a systematic theologian participated in a panel discussion with other colleagues of name and note. The topic, roughly, was a bridge between "theology as a classical discipline" and "theology as lived faith," the means by which faith and practice are bridged and where beliefs find traction within lives of risked discipleship. This person had discerned

10. Morse, *Not Every Spirit*, 13.

11. Ibid., 45–70.

a calling into liturgical service within a historic faith community, after years of teaching and writing in various seminaries. Amidst the additional preparations for this new calling, a conversion experience, of sorts, occurred. "When you pray alongside prisoners, in their own contexts" observed the theologian with quiet intensity, "you think *differently*, theologically." The systematic theologian was discovering (or recalling) what Edward Farley would call the "interpretation of situations"[12]—a way of thinking critically within actual contexts and geographies of lived discipleship that then encourage unpredictable but arguably more rigorous habits of mind for embodied theological reflection. In this unsuspecting conversion, the theologian's disciplinary remove became *theology-in-context*: intimately particular, concretely embodied, unavoidably complex. What had probably been comfortable modes of learning, long before this scholar's formal theological education, returned in all contextual, embodied force within a holy calling. The event and shared reflection simply revealed the unfortunate, systematic abstractions that had been required by specialized, "objective" discipline.

My own introduction to a theology-in-context occurred in a similarly unchosen way. I had completed my Master of Divinity degree and "knew what theology was," in a classical sense. I was asked to reflect theologically on a situation-event in ministry, which I chose as a hospital visit with an older woman who could not speak and could barely hear. I completed the theological reflection as assigned and as I had been trained, identifying the various doctrinal loci evident within this visit and the resulting insights that were to organize the unruly aspects of the relational encounter. As my group pressed my understandings, however, it became very apparent that the use of theology in "theological reflection" within this group was vastly different from how I had been previously trained. Some were even asking questions that seemed rather irrelevant in a classical theological view. "How did you feel God moved in this situation?" I thought human feelings were to be suspect, at least alongside scriptural and theological traditions. "What was the patient's understanding of God?" It was difficult enough to articulate what my own understanding of God is, within scores of traditional voices. How did one identify the God-concept or God-sense of an "other"? "What was God asking of you in this encounter?" I now had less idea about "theol-

12. Farley, *Practicing Gospel*, 29–43.

ogy" than I previously thought. I was about to discover that my training in theology within one community differed vastly from theology as it lived and breathed within another community of discourse. I had been well prepared in the theological tradition within one community, but within its classrooms and texts, I had not been overtly and contextually introduced to the unpredictable and communally-specific life of theology as suggested by another community.

Theology-in-context is the more disciplinary description of what I like to call *artisanal theology*. Both describe the critically reflective yet undeniably storied process begun wherever you are, toward where and whom you (and others) believe God desires you to be. We always seem to begin wherever we are, with whom we understand God to be, going about (conceptually) what we think God desires. Then all these things change, over time, though God's loving and refining pursuit of us does not. This means that theology in your formative community must face theology in others you will encounter with a gentle humility and deep listening for what both communities need to know. My own contexts have predisposed me to a particular kind of theological perspective today—this practical theological perspective—though it is actually an all-encompassing theological task with biblical, historical, systematic, ethical, and constructive dimensions. While cognizant of all this, theology-in-context or an artisanal theology is a bridging-theological artistry that listens to all theological disciplines, as available and pertinent to purpose, while observing situations in which observer and observed participate, co-create, and challenge understanding, interpretation, and wisdom.

Theology-in-context is an embodied way of thinking. It engages all kinds of immediate interactions between persons and settings, with attention and focus, giving them a particular, conceptual shape through critical reflection in community. "Interpretation of situations" is Farley's description to get at a similar notion,[13] but "interpretation" is too easily construed as solely a textual enterprise. There is more to an artisanal theology than interpretation. There are crucial elements beyond textual interpretation for a vibrant life of faith—wonder, risk, celebration, lament, creativity, praise. In disciplinary terms, theology-in-context is yet embodied, exploratory, communal, risky, cross-categorical, and deeply contemplative. Commitment to perspective arises from discomforting

13. Ibid., 29–43.

delight and broadening insight. Like realizing one thinks differently, theologically, when praying alongside prisoners within a penitentiary.

A truly critical theological perspective must arise from exploratory practices of formation, steeped in communal practices of spirit and care that place observer-participants into unsuspected and uncontrollable environments. This takes shape within a disciplined spiritual steward-ship, through accountably covenantal practices begun in humility and lived into communal story through deep listening, covenantal belonging, and spiritual disciplines centered in silence. Personal story shared within covenantal companionship challenges self into greater awareness and ac-ceptance, and places intimate personal discipleship into vulnerable and more receptive spaces whereby encounters with the other and the Holy can happen. God-knowledge then grows within context, self, and other, beyond objective awareness or control. Such God-knowledge then makes its claim to be spoken, to be lived, almost without effort but requiring a demanding willingness. Articulation of the Story compels surrender to story and stories, and to their examination within communal discourses that change the details, sometimes for service of the greater good but sometimes for a sterile emptiness with different lessons.

A Storied View of Theology—Institutions and You

The overwhelming diversity of denominations, faith communities, and contemporary demands make the marketing and participation in one form and format of theology nearly impossible today. As a result, all of us today face the challenge of overwhelming information, personal choice, and hidden influences with respect to understanding what theology is, and how it deepens discipleship in any substantial way. Do you articulate your own theological voice based in your community of origin—church, synagogue, faith community—and its authoritative norms? Do you be-gin by exploring all the options and then see which ones attract you the most? That will be impossible. Is your perspective foreordained? How do you identify your own theological voice within the countless voices and silences you encounter in solid, demanding theological studies? Choice exists, and while I am a firm believer in human agency, many aspects of your own perspective will also arise from your current community's investments and the institutions you choose (or do not choose) for pur-suing your questions and your sense of belonging.

Professed theological perspectives have all kinds of roots—historical, doctrinal, ecclesiological, practical, cultural, and more—and I appreciate what I have learned within each of these lenses. I would like to highlight here one that is often hidden: economic. Some will call this crass, perhaps even unfaithful, but a hidden force within theological learning of all kinds today is the decline of financial and cultural resources (whether perceived or actual) that accompanies a postmodern cultural (ir)relevance. The majority of religious institutions I have had the privilege of observing operate on the basis of a mindset of scarcity. They unintentionally foster an increased competition for declining financial resources. What implicit influences accompany theological perspectives grown within such collective mindsets? Will your theology originate within an organizational culture of material abundance and spiritual poverty or one of spiritual abundance and material poverty?[14] Much of cosmopolitan and media-driven culture thinks little of religion, per se, except as a dangerous force of extremists. What does it mean, then, to articulate a carefully considered, reflectively resourced theological perspective today, steeped within centuries of theological tradition and formed by love and compassion, a just mercy and fierce gentleness? As you discern your own perspective and move toward committing to it in writing, I encourage you to take a hard look at your own communal origins (whether churched or not), the local community in which you live (urban, suburban, rural; cosmopolitan, Midwestern, western, southern, etc.), and the institutions from which you receive resources for your study.

Money shapes institutions of all kinds, and theological ones are no different. I remember finding out, *after* I got ordained into Word and Sacrament ministry, that my tax status had just changed and would cost me $2500 more per year than when I was a happily employed, non-ordained seminary administrator. Ordination by the laying on of hands of my fellow presbyters was a most holy moment in my own story, but it had hidden financial implications never mentioned within any of my previous training. My institution of affiliation was quite pleased with God's actions in this ordination, but it also had a nice benefit for personnel costs in the budget. Never underestimate the pragmatic within

14. High oversimplification here, as spiritual abundance and material poverty don't always go together, nor in reverse. It is an appropriate question, however, for North American contexts—particularly mainline traditions—satiated with material resources yet increasingly hungry for spiritual riches.

the careful stewardship of the transcendent. Always remember: whatever institution you have chosen, whether well-established or newly forming, it is constantly being shaped by its larger institutional ecology—various intersecting worlds of academy, church, tradition, ethnicity-race, local community and more.

Many of you will be drawn to denominationally oriented institutions, such as religiously-committed colleges and seminaries. What is the financial standing and regional or national reach of the institution? Are the more established schools better or just different? For instance, some historically established seminaries have more resources with which to offer degrees of substance, and to keep their promises for well-trained alumnae/i in ministry. Less established or newer institutions have fewer financial resources and a quieter national presence. More established institutions with greater resources are often closer to the national leadership of denominations as well, so they are quite attuned to the ideological and national disputes prevalent within media coverage. That has its advantages. Smaller, less-moneyed institutions living closer to the local community must focus, out of necessity, less on the national disputes or faithful stewardship of plenty, and more on what theological education is to be about in local expression, in order to survive and thrive in a local ecology. In this sense, greater resources result in a greater remove from the contexts and experience required to lead financially struggling faith communities living closer to the cultural wildernesses of our day. Less established or newer institutions will be less nationally recognized, perhaps, but may craft an environment more conducive to "living by faith, not by sight." What does faith mean in an environment where no real financial threats exist, in contrast with institutions that are more regional and close to the lived reality of local faith communities? You must discern, or perhaps in familiar prose, "be as wise as serpents and as innocent as doves." Denominations will also logically foster seminaries who share in the financial viability of the denomination and its historical identity. The preservation of denominational identity as a vested interest of both kinds of institutions suggests that focus will be drawn to denominational identity alongside understandings of gospel, leadership, mission, and more.

Others will be drawn to a university and/or a divinity school for the pursuit of theological knowledge toward lived wisdom. This kind of educational ecology tends to value a more religious-studies, university-discourse perspective, more or less independent of a specific denomina-tional or religious affiliation. These institutions offer a different kind of faithful rhetoric, no less conditioned by economic viability and perspec-tives fostered by a broader wealth of philosophical, scientific, theological, and religious perspectives. Denominational traditions are often noted, but more readily as a historical narrative and less so as an overt partner in financial resourcing. This means that broader cultural resources influ-ence your own awareness and articulated perspective, but a particular denominational tradition may be more skeptical of your institutional loyalties in the search for any professional employment.

Newer communities of intentional covenantal discipleship continue to form and evolve, facing the challenges of communal organizations as any human community must. Small, emerging church communities offer alternative blends of theological perspectives too diverse to qualify eas-ily,[15] except for a forthright commitment to *particular* communities of faith, mission, and discipleship. The large or mega-church organizations that are gaining some public interest are developing their own institu-tions of leadership development. New schools form and then the tasks of critical thinking done at some remove from the immediate demands of risked discipleship result in an uncomfortable divergence of academy from church community. The theological perspectives there demonstrate roots in more contemporary cultural voice or language, such as the popu-lar *The Purpose-Driven Church* by Rick Warren, based upon his leadings at Saddleback Church.[16] However we might describe developing and interactive faith communities with a categorical label—mega-church, emergent, vineyard, etc.—there are more and more developing theologi-cal perspectives coalescing about which you should be aware, even at-tentive and listening. For our purpose of deeper spiritual practice and theological wisdom, what lived expressions of communal commitment undergird each of these theological lenses or "rooms"? Ultimately, theol-ogy is too complex, complicated, and compelling for any homogenous voice, without the prospect of inflicting more damage within already wounded and wounding communities of faith. Your task is to listen as deeply as you can, and be aware of your own received stories lived into your community and institutional ecology.

15. Anderson, *An Emergent Theology for Emerging Churches*; Kimball, *Emerging Church*.

16. Warren, *Purpose-Driven Church*.

Each of the theological windows above offers a particular view, with particular things intended to be within the mind of the viewer. You will feel more drawn to some, and less so to others. Good. Figure out which particular strands of thought Spirit wants you to explore more deeply. Remember: it will take an entire lifetime to explore all those of shared value in your communities of discourse. It will also require careful discrimination and vulnerable judgment. A look at the twentieth century alone shows unspeakable tragedies in name of religious faith. Which windows open onto God's life-affirming good news held in merciful justice? Which windows suggest human violence and oppression or harm of others or the earth? Choose one or two strands of thought in which to begin and listen deeply for threads of grace and healing. Each of these windows offers its own view of the specific doctrinal foci, the systematic and historical ways of understanding God within human individuals and communities. Each one has its own story to tell within the grand fabric of God, a narrative or metanarrative which we can never fully tell or comprehend. Finding your own voice amidst all the other voices and silences presents challenges of integration and creativity. Perhaps a little guidance I wish I had had . . .

FINDING YOUR OWN VOICE

First, proceed assuming that all facets of theology have something to offer faith and service. Folk sayings have it that wisdom comes from your own mistakes in experience. True. But no less true is Otto von Bismarck's impish quip that only fools learn from their own mistakes. "I learn from *other* people's mistakes," he said. Perhaps the lesson is to be about experiencing what you do not believe, only known in your bones by trying to believe it for a while. This does not necessarily change your own belief, but it will help you live alongside and within many more communities of God's cherished creatures. Perhaps the lesson will be about a more gracious and compassionate Presence than you have ever heard possible. We learn from other people's wisdom and gifts too. Delve into the type of theology your own community suspects are "mistaken," or that most contradicts shared expectations. You are both their hope of continuity and the world's promise for compassion lived first within your community and then as a vibrant human interdependence necessary to restore community itself.

Ironically, those that disagree with us the most have the most to teach us.[17] Not necessarily in the content of their theologies or their views of scripture, but in a formative theological learning of enacted humility, unwilled compassion, graced otherness within God's all-encompassing embrace. This means that the task for theology as a way of life within formal theological education is to be a sponge. To soak in everything and all who will comfort and challenge our most treasured ideas. It will only get more ambiguous "out there," as many already know. Better to get accustomed to as broad a view as possible while you are with peers, companions, and mentors who can provide an interpretive framework alongside compassionate companionship.

If you are Christian, spend prayerful, contemplative time with as many self-identified Christians as possible, alternating between historical and contemporary voices—ancient, African, medieval, Asian, Renaissance, European, Reformation, North American, Enlightenment, Hispanic, and more. Read works from those whom you are afraid of hearing truth in love—Catholic, if you are Protestant; female, if you are male; black, if you are white; conservative, if you are liberal; homosexual, if you are straight, poor if you are materially rich. The best of any classical tradition, when truly explored, will come to life when read alongside contemporary voices who speak a different language than you want to hear. As you become more attuned to your own faith identity, then branch out into even more practices. Stephen Prothero has argued that the United States is simultaneously the most religious nation in the developing world—in terms of religiosity or belief in all things supernatural—*and* the most religiously ignorant, not only about other religions, plural, but also about what they are supposed to believe.[18] Deep listening requires openness, patience, and even exploration of perspectives and practices that can shape your discipleship more sensitive to the contexts where theology is living today.

Particular faith identities, of course, inform theological understanding. Why *are* you United Methodist, or Presbyterian, or Baptist, or AME, or UCC, or Free Church, or unchurched or . . . ? Each of us receives an identity, or a variety of identities, from the settings of our birth, early life, or recent history. There's not one right answer here, and our felt-sense

17. Wheeler, "Strangers: A Dialogue about the Church."
18. Prothero, *Religious Literacy*, 26.

may differ from what our communities observe. Some answers are better than others, however, and by that I mean knowing your own identity as it grows and why. My own identity has grown increasingly complex, multi-traditional, and coherently fragmented, which is so very postmodern of me. I grew up Presbyterian because my Baptist and Brethren parents liked the minister of the Presbyterian Church. That was my beginning. I felt at home for a long time in my Presbyterian identity—strong intellect, high verbal needs, familiar hymns, familiar liturgy. For just as long, I had no critically reflective reasons for why I was Presbyterian. I had to learn the tradition's felt identity from my theological studies, from some of my professors, from other students, from the denomination that provided some background for passing the ordination exams. As I studied and learned, I realized that I felt at home here because of many things—sovereignty of God emphasis, confessional tradition, strong tradition of education and preaching, and familiar colleagues with whom I strengthened this Presbyterian identity. It didn't hurt that two of my uncles, one of whom was greatly important for my own intellectual development, were Presbyterian too. So, amidst prayerful discernment and practical detail, I pursued my calling into deeper learning in the Presbyterian Church USA, being ordained to Word and Sacrament ministry in May 2002.

My own story and physical body are rooted in this one historical tradition, but the world of spirit is much larger than any one denominational community. Therein lies a challenge, particularly for those trying to find their own voices amidst previous generations of thought. Professional identity rooted in a historical tradition needs both to witness from personal experience within one tradition *and* to risk surrender to the sovereignty of the Holy within a *diversity* of Christian traditions, let alone others. I do not presume to know why God works through multiple denominations and even various faiths. I do know that my own Presbyterian identity has been deepened and strengthened by intimate explorations in many communities of spiritual practice. I find that being in other traditions allows me to know my own Reformed bones better, more intimately. My trust of God grows the more regularly I see obvious fruits of the Spirit in traditions and places that are not Presbyterian in the least. So my own Presbyterian sense of spirit has been deepened and nuanced by the Lutherans (ECLA), Episcopalians, Roman Catholics (orders more than dioceses), Quakers (Society of Friends), Church of the Brethren, Jews, and even a Buddhist sangha in a town close to where

I live. Any theology-in-context I articulate in writing or speech today would not be remotely the one I struggled to name at the conclusion of my formal learning, but my voice and Presbyterian identity are more deeply rooted in scriptural and theological interpretations of radical covenant lived into my own story. My communities of discernment were crucial for this theology-in-context, but they also required a resilience of me that comes only when one is open to being shaped by others' stories and the Story of God yet untold.

COMMUNAL DISCERNMENT

Covenantal communities today, whether living into a rhetorical understanding of "covenant" or sustaining the vibrant claim and conflict of covenant itself, contribute the necessary crucible in which personal truths become communal truths resonant with the Story of God. In other words, prepare to have your buttons pushed on at least one occasion as you deepen your spiritual practice. Learn more and more ways to respond gracefully and openly to this experience. Your spiritual demeanor, as expressed in your body language and in your integrated wisdom, will serve you well, *if* you have risked engagement in formation and you submit to the possibility that everyone has something to contribute to your own understandings. For example, my candidacy review on the floor of presbytery was the proscribed telling of my faith story and a first reading of my faith statement. I experienced it as an incredibly uplifting and remarkable opportunity to celebrate what I had experienced, what I was learning about my own vocational pursuits. Others saw the exchange in vastly different hues of emotion and threat. Both views offer a truth to hear.

As fairly typical of this process, someone on the floor asked about my experience of confirmation class and baptism when I was twelve years old. I was quite frank about its meaninglessness for me at the time, its developmentally inappropriate timing for my own journey. I was apparently too frank for the comfort of some. A minister member of presbytery was clearly offended by my seemingly casual account of something like confirmation class and baptism. He asked, "Was there ever a time when you professed faith in Jesus Christ and actually meant it?" My friends had to tell me later about the patronizing and disrespectful tone, because I honestly did not hear it at the time. I responded with great tenderness about a time when I was sitting at the kitchen table with my mother, a Presbyterian elder, who listened to me complain about the unreality of confirmation, its utter lack of meaning for me in the eighth grade. She asked me whether my experience was any different now, especially as I was nearing college. I told her, "Yes, quite different." She asked me the Presbyterian questions for a profession of faith, and I responded that night with my first body-felt profession of faith in Jesus Christ. It was a delight to be able to remember that occasion aloud with minister and elder members of my faith community, and it was a nice, if unplanned, tribute to my mother in a setting of personal and professional impor-tance. It was only afterwards that my friends asked me whether I was angry about that minister member's question and tone. I was perplexed and asked them to describe it, as I had not experienced it that way at all.

Reflecting on this experience from this point in my life, with inten-tional formation in view, I think human abilities to respond non-anx-iously, honestly, and with integrity to experience root in a true desire to discern with community about our intimate stories and paths of disciple-ship. If there are those in the "community" who really observe an unfit-ness between our path and that of the tradition, then it is better to know that as early as possible. Here I am *not* talking about public discourse, in general. This openness may not aid a fierce theological compassion against the horrific realities of systemic oppressions in global humanity, whether based in race, ethnicity, access to resources, gender, and more. But within religious communities today, already so fragmented and frag-menting, I have found that if God does intend a certain path, then doors open. If another path leads to greater receptivity of gifts and talents, then that is a better path.

True discernment within seeking communities of radical covenant is lived in a willingness to face up to the consequences of unexpected bumps in the road. If discernment originates in your own intent—how-ever explicit or implicit—to try to get the right answer, to say the right thing, to be the right kind of Christian or Jew or Muslim, then the path will be fraught with insecurity, distress and frustration. Faithful disciples of any broader faith tradition will hear your fear, your uncertainty, your own lack of trust in them to listen alongside you. They will encourage you, in ways that will feel really uncomfortable, to deepen your trust that God is leading your footsteps. If you do not trust your body of faith now, you will not grow in intimacy within it, nor be able to contribute your gifts there in the future.

CONCLUSION

In sum, a theology-in-context that becomes truly artisanal—your own blend of covenantally companioned and rooted tradition, expressed with a discerned artistry enlightened with delight—will be planted, nurtured, refined and committed at the creative, communal crux in which solidity yet difficulty are assured. Crucible might be a better word for the discerning energies involved. Preacher and homiletics professor Fred Craddock describes the predictable dynamic at this place, the historical relationship of any faith tradition doing the work of its "traditioning" from one generation to the next. "A church is born and it grows. Grows so much that it decides to start a school in order to prepare its leaders for future generations. The excitement is palpable as it gathers a faculty and a board of trustees, and then calls a principal or a dean. The dean goes into her office, sits at her newly varnished desk placed for the work of educational administration, and opens the mail. On the top of the pile lies a letter from one of the local churches saying, "We don't like what you're doin' down there."[19] It never fails, a felt gap between intentional, formal learning, removed for reflective study, and the lived practice of local congregations. It is a gift in disguise, though one remembers this better on some days than on others. Ultimately, it is this oven that will fire your own vision, your own practice, your part in the unfolding Story of God.

19. Craddock, "In the Service of the Gospel," *McCord Public Lecture Series*.

5

An Artisanal Theological Loaf

My theology begins within the fold of Presbyterian Christianity (PCUSA), and blossoms out into numerous strands of God's unpredictable and great Tree of Life. An Ohioan, small-town, Presbyterian pastor named the delights and, unexpectedly, the challenges in his local congregation, such that my Brethren and Baptist Christian parents could perceive a calling to membership in that local congregation. We became Presbyterian Christians. Whether members of my "church family" call it God's providence, or agnostic friends see an event of chance and circumstance, does not really concern me anymore. My roots are Presbyterian Christian. Even so, the various "worlds" shaping my experience divide my being into at least two, even three or more parts: mind, body, spirit. In that paradigm, God's work with one dimension of being human often supersedes awareness of God's work in the others. My mind and body became aware of and active in my faith much later than my spirit, in Spirit, at my baptism.[1]

This entrance into a Presbyterian Christian identity and historical community took root formally during my eighth-grade year, upon God's action in my baptism and my first public profession of faith. That was the public and communal act of God within my life. *I* knew myself to be a disciple of Jesus Christ, intimately, only when I sat with my mother at the kitchen table, many years later, close to college. In response to her elder-stewardship of this theological tradition, I answered the same "profession of faith" questions within the *Book of Order*. I felt whole in my path of Christian curiosity, at that point. And I learned that my spirit is

---

1. Note the implicit communication here that my entire theological perspective rests in the sacrament of baptism, the beginning of vocation in Reformed theological language.

often years ahead of the rest of me, which is not an uncommon phenomenon. More recently, however, my body guides and teaches me in God's intentions, gifts, and callings. Of course, I still spend the most amount of time listening to my mind and trying to understand before risking faith outwardly. I am Presbyterian, after all, and this theological tradition clearly abides by Anselm's *fides quaerens intellectum*, or "faith seeking understanding."[2]

This theological statement will address, in theological perspectives resonant with Reformed theological voices, the roots, tensions, and views that undergird my own pursuits of theological wisdom in spiritual practice and professional ministry.[3] The *roots* show my own lived assumptions, some confirmed, some challenged, as my practices have deepened through years of ministry service. Two related *tensions* become apparent in a poem I wrote, exploring order and disorder, decency and indecency, as I experience it within my own faith journey in Reformed theological communities. The theological *views* on which my ministry rests were shaped most recently within an intentional and critical process of ministry formation, but they now inform my perspectives clear back to my origins.

Allow me to offer a concise summary of theological views, as they inform all that is to come. I accept the Christian scriptures to be by the Spirit a unique and authoritative witness to Jesus Christ, revealing the relational Life of God in the power of the Spirit as a loving, dancing, overwhelming Three-in-One, Triune God. I minister in obedience to Christ, as instructed by the received Word and confessions of the PCUSA, as governed by its polity and discipline. The church lives as the Body of Christ, both-as-one, enlivening and interweaving fallen historical traditions with the disruptive, holy path of compassionate justice, cruciform love, energetic service, reconciling peace, and unifying purity. Christ-like leadership is that which moves the church-Body forward within increasing missional clarity toward the reign of God, promised and present. Ordained leadership within the PCUSA is to function alone, without any ontological presuppositions or alterations of the human person: (1) deacon ordination to ministries of pastoral care, congregational visitation,

2. Migliore, *Faith Seeking Understanding*, 2.

3. Note "resonant with" in this opening thesis statement. This allows me to incorporate other theological voices that have spoken to me, yet are not denominationally identified as I am.

outreach mission, liturgical service; or (2) presbyter ordination (either as minister of Word and Sacrament or as governing elder) to ministries of (elder) governance, care, outreach-mission, liturgy; and (W&S) ministries of teaching, preaching, and the right administration of the sacraments of Baptism and Communion. All Presbyterians are ministers of the Gospel. The roots and tensions, with their importance further revealed in covenantal, critical reflection, begin the development of this theological perspective.[4]

ROOTS

My pursuit of wisdom in spiritual practice and Christian ministry is rooted and nourished in an embodied trust in the sovereignty of God and God's participatory creativity to redeem and sanctify all events—intended and unintended, willed and unwilled—within an unpredictable, life of discipleship (Rom 8:28). This trust in God's Presence formed in early experiences in nature, in theological conversations with my father (he used to invite me to read short classics and then we would go out to breakfast to talk about them), in my mother's deep listening and lived faith through service in family and local community, in my one sister's tumultuous entrance into her understanding of religious faith. The trust was lived actively into my own life during years of teaching junior high at a girls' school in Pasadena, California. I heard a woman pastor preach, joined the church of my own volition (with conditions of a one-year membership, before departure and proof of my written statement and then-conviction, "the church was irreparably fallen and useless"), and was repeatedly drawn into times with God through reading theology, lay service, worship, and liturgical ritual. God is present (John 1:14). I observed the lived trust of others within God's church, especially those who could articulate God's sovereignty and suffering within (and because of) the Body of Christ. In a rose-tinted idealism, I pursued this trust further into formal theological education where my world was shaken and stretched, enlivened and deepened, wounded and healed beyond all imagination.

4. Note the opening and closing sentences to this paragraph: it communicates a concise summary is coming, then concludes summary with transition to next section of the paper. Also notice the major doctrinal points referenced, important for certification boards: Triune doctrine of God with centrality through Jesus Christ, authority of scriptures, understanding of church-Body (with implicit statements on sovereignty and sin to come), leadership, and then ordination within this theological tradition.

I found myself as an ordained minister within the Presbyterian Church (USA), only to be taught most intimately, most dearly, by non-ordained Christian disciples and agnostic, even atheist, seekers. God is present (John 1:14). This root awareness amidst both pain and pleasure allows faithful weathering of things unimagined and unspoken.

This trust is embodied today in two ways. The first is through regular but varying spiritual practices, traditioned by my Presbyterian community and invited by companions I have met along the way. For example, I understand my faith life within daily prayer and a weekly Sabbath practice, shared with (and held accountable by) my spiritual friend and husband, whereby we are enlivened and challenged in Spirit's leading to deep listening, healthy vulnerability, and liturgical prayer. Trust is embodied in a second sense of "knowing deeply within my body," not in spoken words or articulate doctrines. The Quaker practice of centering down and meditatively seeking God's light within a listening contemplation shapes my seeing in addition to my knowing. God "speaks" to me within unspoken sensation. The Spirit leads me to know undying and overwhelming love, gentle reprimand, merciful justice, reconciliation and redemption. I know I have been justified within the work of Christ, and my life is being sanctified in the jumps, stops, and starts it needs. This trust is articulately informed and challenged by an ecumenical, Reformed theology—Reformed and always reforming, rooted but moving outward from a narrow Presbyterianism into ecumenical and even interfaith communities. John Calvin's kind of theology, there, with respect to knowing who is "in God's church."[5] My trust in the human body far exceeds Calvin's, but this is a customary divergence from most men of faith whom I have read and those whom I know.

TENSIONS

I wrote a poem to get at the rub between my spirit, mind, and body—this rootedness in a "decent and orderly" tradition such as the Presbyterian

---

5. "For here we are not bidden to distinguish between reprobate and elect—that is for God alone, not for us to do—but to establish with certainty in our hearts that all those who, by the kindness of God the Father, through the working of the Holy Spirit have entered into fellowship with Christ . . . " Calvin, *Institutes of the Christian Religion*, 1015–16. This extends even to attempts to distinguish those who profess Christ by name from those who do not say Christ, but who do his work (Matt 21:28ff).

Church (USA)[6] that is yet moving outward with the good news that can actually find the lost and feed the hungry, wherever they may be found and fed.

> Decently and in order
> What kind of order?
> What kind of decency?
> We know so little.
>
> Feed the lost
> Lose the hungry
> That's what we do
> With mismatched grace
>
> Considered response in
> A disordered order.
> Indecent decency for life
> All seem to want
>
> Because so few have it
> Few spirits survive it
> Unseen cuffs, slap of privilege
> What, with sorrow?
>
> Find the lost
> Feed the hungry
> Love beyond knowing,
> We know only All.

The tension between an orderly "tradition," as a noun, and the life of God it means to "tradition," as a verb, courses through this theology, practice, and ministry. A tradition's orderliness authentically grounds all recalcitrant faithful, even amidst the unavoidable holy disorder that re-

---

6. First Corinthians 14:40 is a Presbyterian mantra, "all things should be done decently and in order."

sults within a life governed by the power of the Spirit. There is a decency to a graced, God-professed-good life, grounded in search of the sacred, that is made indecent in "safe religion," which trusts God so little that it attempts to force Spirit to speak within rigidly defined human boxes. Or even texts.

It is in this tension that I challenge—along with many others, supported especially by *The Confession of 1967*—some aspects of commonly held Reformed theology.[7] A staid understanding of the utter depravity[8] or sinfulness of humankind, for instance. Or a Reformed understanding of God's sovereignty,[9] at least as we think of power in our human worlds, power "over" or "against." Instead, I profess human sinfulness as descriptive and articulate of reality—thoroughly comprehensive—but not determinative within God's irrepressible agency.[10] I push against what "utter" means. Karl Barth wrote that "to be human is to be with God. . . . Godlessness is not, therefore, a possibility, but an ontological impossibility for humanity. . . . Sin is undoubtedly committed and exists. Yet sin itself is not a possibility but an ontological impossibility for humanity."[11] Sinfulness is not what I dispute, but utter sinfulness as a cop-out against lived human freedom and active agency, accountable to God-given gifts.

I also profess divine sovereignty as a Chosen, compassionate mutuality, a God-enacted rhythm of submission and assertion that creates relationship.[12] Even with those who choose against such Spirit, this sovereignty shows an implicit, holding love. Walter Brueggemann unearths this very witness from earliest scriptural texts with Judeo-Christian scripture. As he describes it, "the category of sovereignty and obedience is a crucial and definitional mark of humans. . . . Being birthed into Yahweh's creation brings the human person under the rule of the Sovereign who

7. This is place where, in my own voice, I can honor my tradition yet contribute to it, from within my own experience. This shows knowledge of tradition, and commitment to work within it as God so leads, known in conscience and communal discernment.

8. *Book of Confessions* 5.036–5.038 (Second Helvetic Confession); 6.034 (Westminster Confession).

9. *Book of Confessions* 6.011 and 6.112 (Westminster Confession); 7.052 (The Shorter Catechism); 7.220, 7.262, 7.306 etc. (The Larger Catechism).

10. *Book of Confessions* 9.12–9.19.

11. Barth, *Karl Barth*, 230–32. Excerpt reprinted from Barth, *Church Dogmatics* III/2, 135–36.

12. *Book of Confessions* 9.15, 9.17 (Confession of 1967); 10.3 (Brief Statement, line 29).

creates."[13] Brueggemann's second and third marks of divine-human covenantal relationship—God's fidelity from compassion and a rhythm of mutuality—are discovered within the trust and vulnerability that come with sovereignty/obedience. [14] The sovereignty of God and the obedient human creature are woven into authentically free relationship by means of God's compassionate fidelity, in contrast to worldly perceptions of obedience to will or authoritarian power. God's compassion is such that covenantal relationship identified by sovereignty and obedience is yet lived from a source of pathos, care, and mercy. God's power "with" has absolutely no resemblance, therefore, to power "over" or power "against." Reformed theology built upon a tensive dynamism between humanly determinative order and sacredly empowered disorder, polite-social decency and holy enacted indecency, undergirds both of these challenges. This perspective claims utter human depravity within its historical witness, even as it also shows challenge to human abuse of the doctrinal description. It rests wholly within the sovereignty of God, yet not in a fashion sensible to human understandings of power.[15]

VIEWS

No theological statement can really give adequate voice to ongoing learning in faith, reformed and reforming within the patient grace of God. With intentional formation for religious service and leadership in mind, I will touch upon a view of God's Triunity; the scriptures as a unique and authoritative witness to Jesus Christ; God's church as both the Body of Christ and a fallen institution continually redeeming and being redeemed; Christlike leadership within this Body-church; and the understanding of ordination within my particular community of faith, the Presbyterian Church (USA). These summary views have emerged from my own story, my deepened practice within covenantal communities, and my continuing engagement with theological scholarship.

13. Brueggemann, *Theology of the Old Testament*, 409.

14. Ibid., 454ff.

15. Notice the summary conclusion of this section where the resources brought to bear are within my tradition, which I then interpret with a personal judgment. The task here is to weave traditional and complementary resources into your own thinking, offering a living perspective within your tradition and with voices that complement or challenge such tradition "as written."

God's Triunity

A primarily relational understanding of God informs my theological perspective and pursuit of wisdom in the practice of ministry.[16] As covenant is interwoven throughout the scriptural narrative, [17] so do I know its meaning in my own life from the faithfulness of God in spiritual companions and community.[18] I understand human relationship to be only a glimpse of grace intended and received, lived in full within the Trinity who creates, redeems, and sustains.[19] Dorothy Sayers summarizes best how futile a description of the Trinity is within human prose. In "Scalene Trinities," she observes the reality of God's Triunity to be an equilateral triangle, perfect and imaginable within the Idea. Any human writer attempting to articulate co-creative and participatory Love, however, as it flows and dances unhindered within the three-yet-one "relationality" of Father, Son, and Holy Spirit, winds up with a scalene trinity, at best. Overemphasizing one side, to the inaccuracy of the other Two.[20]

With that caveat, my understanding of God's Triunity arises from a sense of the sacred larger than any one scriptural witness, yet inarticulately available within contemplation and deep listening between vulnerable covenantal companions. God as Three-in-One, made available in the life, death, and new life of Jesus Christ in the power of the Spirit, continues to create, provoke, disturb, comfort, and care for those open to the least, last, and lost. Those who challenge conviction either in their own rigid beliefs, or with their very presence in my life, demand a lived trust into deeper understanding. I see Spirit most easily in the lives of those who invite the unsuspecting Stranger into their lives, in deeper encounter with gospel witness, without words. Sheep and goats cannot be distinguished by *us*, after all.[21] Innumerable ministry events have shaped

16. See Loder and Neidhardt, *Knight's Move*.

17. Gen 6:18, 9:9, 15:18, 17:2; Exod 19:5; Ps 25:14; 89:3; Matt 26:28; Luke 1:72; Acts 7:8; Rom 11:27; 2 Cor 3:6–14; Heb 7:22, 12:24.

18. *Book of Confessions* 3.21 (The Scots Confession); 4.019, 074, 079, 082, 4.101 (The Heidelberg Catechism); 5.126, 5.154, 5.187, 5.192 (The Second Helvetic Confession); 6.037–042, 6.055, 6.080 (Westminster Confession) 7.286 (The Larger Catechism); 9:18, 9.28 (Confession of 1967); 10.3 (Brief Statement, line 42, 48).

19. The Introduction to the *Book of Confessions* states, "All confessions explicitly or implicitly confess the doctrine of the Trinity" (xvii).

20. Sayers, *Mind of the Maker*, 149ff.

21. Matt 25:31–46.

this awareness—both at the lively intersection of life and death at the side of a hospital or Hospice bed, and as I minister with colleagues, lay and ordained, in the service of local congregations.

I know God's Triunity when I hold a tradition's doctrine loosely enough to listen to a practitioner of any faith tradition teach or speak of a just compassion. Looking for Christ in the face of those who do not speak his name has repeatedly surprised me with holy encounters with the person of Christ, recognizable in discernment with Christian companions and the witness of scripture. I know God's primary relationality when old wounds are healed in the most unexpected and gracious fashion. My own capacity for intense feeling and inarticulate intuition has been healed by a Presbyterian laywoman and confirmed within spiritual direction. I have affirmed countless young and older women in their own healthy expression of anger—at wounds received, at prejudice, at unjust limitation of expression—such that they could offer it as healing salves to their communities and to themselves as prophetic energies for communal education and co-creation of new life for outreach and mission. Spirit continues to sanctify all parts of human experience, toward the reign of God, now and not yet.

I realize that scripture does not articulate a doctrine of the Trinity. The historically diverse Christian church has, then and now. But this flowing, dancing, unpredictable, yet trustworthy relationality promises (and delivers) a rootedness previously unimagined, a groundlessness necessary for being an authentic human being (i.e., a creature, obedient to Creator), and an overflowing affection (*caritas*) for friend and foe alike. God as Triunity roots, convicts, justifies, and sanctifies unfinished human creatures to their fully alive state with God. Truly human.

Scriptures

I accept the Christian scriptures to be a unique and authoritative witness to Jesus Christ, who makes God known in the power of the Spirit.[22] The Christian "canon" is that traditioned vehicle of the journeys of God's people, many and one. I do not think the canon or any scriptures outside

---

22. Migliore, *Faith Seeking Understanding.* See esp. chapter 3, "The Authority of Scripture." My ability to read this standard text with critical and reconstructive eyes has clearly been shaped by Fiorenza, *Bread Not Stone.* See also Barth, *Church Dogmatics* I/2, 457ff.

the Protestant canon can limit God's continued speaking and revelations, however.[23] The doctrinal paradigm, the Bible as the Word of God, is an important contribution to my faith community's understanding of its theological past.[24] I profess this to be true, but only as Christ lives cruciform love and seeds of grace into the lives of readers, listeners, and scholars alike. The Bible itself is a book without any mystical powers of its own, or of its own accord. The key, it seems to me, is the *living* Word, Christ lived in-me-and-not-me, not a highly literate attempt to abstract and control who God loves or how we are to live this love into risked discipleship for a just liberation and reconciling peace for all. The historical paradigm, the Bible as solely a historical document for historical-critical analysis, corrects many of the abuses a solely-doctrinal tidiness has inflicted upon the lives of discipleship of many traditions—Christian, but certainly Jewish, Islamic, and more. It may strip the life of the faith community away, however, with a razor-sharp precision never intended for Trinitarian relational creation and sustenance.[25] Kierkegaard muses a poetic truth here: some things are true when whispered, yet become false when shouted.[26] Historical-critical scholarship is a crucial tool for heightened human awareness, critique, and creativity, but taken at a shout, or as *the* path of interpretation, it misses the primarily relational point of full humanity.

The pastoral-theological paradigm that Elisabeth Schüssler Fiorenza proposes, [27] as integration of the first two, sustains a creative tension between the pastoral situation and its theological response. Within this paradigm, finding root in unsuspected places within academy and emerging churches, the Bible demonstrates a root-model for the Christian Church. Instead of doctrinal or historical-critical criteria, this new root-model discerns revelation within scriptural witness, as Schüssler Fiorenza de-

23. Exod 3, "I am who I will be," and Gal 3:28–29. *Book of Confessions* 8.11 (Theological Declaration of Barmen); 9.27–29 (Confession of 1967); 10.4 (Brief Statement lines 60–61).

24. *Book of Confessions* 3.18 (Scots Confession); 4.103 (The Heidelberg Catechism); 5.003 (The Second Helvetic Confession); 6.002 (Westminster Confession); 7.114 (The Larger Catechism);

25. *Book of Confessions* 9.29 (Confession of 1967): "The church, therefore, has an obligation to approach the Scriptures with literary and historical understanding."

26. Søren Kierkegaard, cited by Craddock, *McCord Lecture Series.*

27. Schüssler Fiorenza, *Bread Not Stone*, esp. chapter 2, "For the Sake of Our Salvation: Biblical Interpretation and the Community of Faith."

scribes it, for the sake of our salvation. She defines her term salvation as total human salvation and wholeness, not just "the soul"—liberation from social and political oppression, not just truth revealed in the far-off Reign of God.[28] Thomas Merton gives a compelling description of salvation as well, resonant with Schüssler Fiorenza's tradition and my own perspective.

> Salvation is an objective and mystical reality—the finding of ourselves in Christ, in the Spirit, or, if you prefer, in the supernatural order of nature. This includes and sublimates and perfects the natural self-realization which it to some extent presupposes, and usually effects, and always transcends. Therefore this discovery of ourselves is always a losing of ourselves—a death and a resurrection. . . . The discovery of ourselves in God, and of God in ourselves, by a charity that also finds all other men in God with ourselves is, therefore not the discovery of ourselves but of Christ."[29]

What this means is that I accept scripture to be a unique and authoritative witness to Jesus Christ who saves, but I also continue to be saved as I meet the living Word in unexpected, humbling, and life-giving encounters. I listen to these situations, these encounters, deeply and within faithful covenants and practices of worship. Scripture is an authoritative witness, within faith community, that allows me to recognize the fingerprints of God in my own faith experience. It offers regular confirmation and challenge toward what the Spirit of God urges for interpretation, understanding, and lived discipleship today.

God's Church

Christian traditions describe the marks of God's church from the Niceno-Constantinopolitan creed, "We believe in one holy catholic and apostolic church."[30] The institution of the Christian Church lives a vibrant tradition as it wrestles with intentions around *one, holy, catholic,* and *apostolic.*

28. Schüssler Fiorenza, *Bread Not Stone*, 36–41.

29. Merton, *No Man is an Island*, xiv–xv. Of interest is the omission of the word "salvation" from the Confessions between The Larger Catechism (*Book of Confessions* 7.305) until A Brief Statement (10.4). This may create unspoken misunderstandings, so this approach to scripture also intends to heighten awareness of the theological reality of salvation, lived today.

30. *Book of Confessions*, 1.3.

Furthermore, the historical church has demonstrated a variety of expressions throughout the centuries: militant and triumphant, visible and invisible.[31] Within this heritage, I understand God's church to be both the visible Body of Christ, those communities in which the gospel is truly preached and the sacraments are rightly administered,[32] and the invisible Body of Christ, all those unexpected gatherings and companionships in which risked discipleship grows, the fruits of the Spirit can be found, and cruciform vulnerable love binds all toward mutual joy and hope for all. A colleague once argued, quite convincingly, that works' righteousness does not apply to children of God, as each is a child of God by grace in faith, but the church is only the church in what it does. If risked discipleship does not grow, if fruits of the Spirit cloy at the ground, if hospitable welcome and cruciform love do not show forth shoots of new life, then questions grow in my spirit toward the Body's call for me into new life.[33]

Regardless of ecclesial standing or legitimation—which does not protect human knowledge from the refining fire of a living Lord—I suggest that the church lives as the Body of Christ, both-as-one, in which God enlivens and interweaves fallen historical traditions with the disruptive, holy path of compassionate justice, cruciform love, energetic service, reconciling peace, and unifying purity.[34] Avery Dulles offers his classic views on the models of church: institution, mystical communion, sacrament, herald, servant, community of disciples.[35] W. Paul Jones eschews dividing the church into various models by arguing for internal diversity within every congregation, consisting of various worldviews: separation and reunion, conflict and vindication, emptiness and fulfillment, condemnation and forgiveness, suffering and endurance.[36] My own tradition names

31. McKim, *Introducing the Reformed Faith*, 125. "The church militant is the visible Christian church on Earth. The church triumphant is the church in heaven composed of all who have died and share in the reality of heaven. . . . The 'visible' church is the outward, organized church on Earth that is apparent. . . . The 'invisible church' is the body of genuine believe in Christ on Earth and in heaven. They may or may not be directly associated with a visible body of believers."

32. *Book of Confessions* 5.124–41 (The Second Helvetic Confession); 6.140–45 (Westminster Confession).

33. *Book of Confessions* 9.31 (Confession of 1967).

34. Ibid., 9.34.

35. Avery Dulles, *Models of the Church*, cited in McKim, 127–28.

36. Jones, *Worlds Within a Congregation*. See esp. chapter 4, the Theological Worlds Inventory (TWI).

the great ends of the church in the *Book of Order*, G-1.0200: proclamation of the gospel for the salvation of humankind; the shelter, nurture, and spiritual fellowship of the children of God; the maintenance of divine worship; the preservation of the truth; the promotion of social righteousness; and the exhibition of the Kingdom of Heaven to the world.[37]

Scripture describes the Church of God as the people of God, originating from earliest etymologies within Judeo-Christian scriptures naming "a gathered assembly" for worship or an *ecclesia*. God's people are those chosen within covenantal promise to live God's love into the world. Karl Barth argues that God chose all of humankind in the Word of God, lived into time in Jesus of Nazareth, continuing to break into our world(s) in the power of the Spirit.[38] The themes of covenant and election intertwine throughout this definition of the Church as God's people, early origins within Hebrew traditions, reformed and reforming for Christians in the life, death, and resurrection of Jesus Christ. The Church, therefore, is Christ's Body made real in this world. No less true is the church as a fallen human institution, forever being sanctified within the work of the Holy Spirit.[39] This fallenness actually makes the gracious deliverance of God in the power of the Spirit more tangible, more real, and a more powerful witness in the end. The reality of the church lives on in its both-and Body-and-being, moved closer and closer to God's purposes in the power of the Spirit and led-followed-led by religious leadership, so called by the Body-church.

Christ-like leadership

As summarized above, Christ-like leadership is that which moves the people of God forward within an increasing missional clarity, regardless of ordination or ontological status, toward the reign of God, promised and present.[40] The reign of God, while completely indescribable, yet shows forth glimpses within Christian traditions of Jesus' life: preaching

---

37. Note reliance upon Reformed documentation, in this case, the Presbyterian Church (USA) constitution.

38. Barth, *Church Dogmatics* II/2, 3ff.

39. Reno, *In the Ruins of the Church*; Soelle, *Theology for Skeptics*; and Spong, *Why Christianity Must Change or Die*.

40. *Book of Confessions* 9.31–33 (Confession of 1967).

the good news to the poor and releasing those in bondage, teaching by word and deed and blessing, healing the sick, bearing pain of the broken-hearted, communing with outcasts, forgiving sins, and calling all to repentance and faith.[41] All those who urge and encourage others toward this life of compassion, expressive delight in the gifts of God, openness to the Spirit for particular callings of faith, are leaders of the faith community. The communion of saints, another Reformed emphasis for perceiving the present-and-past people of God,[42] offers ready ministers of the gospel, though the church in its fallen communal life remains unaware of the unending resources at its collective fingertips.

CONCLUSION

The "loaf" given expression here does have its shape, texture, and particular nuances within prose and poetry. It begins with my particular narrative and extends through that particularity into encounter with scripture, lived experience of communal belonging and struggle, theological resourcing, and formal categories of theological understanding. Its contribution or participation in the broader Story of God, however, really depends upon how it is shared, whom it reaches and for what purpose, how its digestion furthers (or stymies) a broader movement toward what Christian traditions call the reign of God—good news for the poor, release from bondage, generosity of blessing, healing the sick, bearing pain of the broken-hearted, communing with outcasts, forgiveness of sin, and calling all to repentance and faith. The danger at this stage of theological articulation is thinking that the product has been the point.

Whether the product is understood here as deeper practice, a degree, a professional certification, or a vocational employment, the distinctive orientation of a truly artisanal theology presses beyond this product into a necessary but often spontaneous question of shared delight—of grace and fidelity, satisfaction and imagination, daring self-assertion and gra-

41. Placher and Willis-Watkins, *Belonging to God*. Another volume with more Baptist roots describes the Kingdom of God as the Nu Jeruz, a neologism taken from rap music. See Corbitt and Nix-Early, *Taking It to the Streets*.

42. *Book of Confessions* 2.3 (The Apostle's Creed); 4.023, 4.055 (The Heidelberg Catechism); 5.125 (The Second Helvetic Confession); 6.146–47 (Westminster Confession); 7.173 (The Larger Catechism); 10.5 (Brief Statement, line 77).

cious self-reception able to companion suffering and proclaim the good news, which truly liberates human persons into a covenantal interdependence previously unimagined.

Epilogue

Expressive delight threatens most of us, believe it or not. I learned this unexpectedly from author and artist Julia Cameron, most known for her book, *The Artist's Way: a Spiritual Path to Higher Creativity*. I came across her work when I needed to write an original dissertation proposal. Being a Type A achiever, I researched and purchased a book on creativity in order to learn all about it. What I did not count on was the holy havoc that engaged delight would ultimately wreak in my own life: a daringly creative proposal, fresh perceptions on the reality of sin not as moral category but as lived resistance to grace, a spectacular romance that took my breath away into ultimately a wedding, and more. If the graces had not been so numerous, so impossible to deny and strengthening of my own awareness of Grace personified, my frail spirit would never have chosen or thought such delight possible. Marianne Williamson nailed it right on the head in words oft-quoted, even by Nelson Mandela. Our greatest fear is not that we are inadequate, small or powerless, but that we are powerful beyond measure. "It is our light," she said, "not our darkness, that most frightens us."[1] Any theological wisdom to be shared in generations to come—the fruits received and shared from within and beyond an artisanal theology—must express this kind of light, this kind of expressive delight within the bones and eyes of those who would speak true.

The threat can be felt most acutely in institutions of authority and with things we hold to be most sacred. Cameron tells a great story of teaching creativity at a prestigious university, and bumping into a scholar coming down the stairs while she was heading up the stairs. He asked her about whose creativity she studied, "Whose theories?" he asked. "I was wondering whose theories you enjoy?" When she responded with her

---

1. Williamson, *Return to Love*, 190–91.

own delight in creativity itself—the artistry of engaged life and practice—he was befuddled and said, "Oh dear. Well, lovely to meet you."[2] Cameron suggests that those who build things and those who take them apart will always go in separate directions. "The energy of construction and the energy of deconstruction feel very different, although both are energies of discernment, although both ask the question, 'What if . . . ?'"[3] Somewhat in contrast to her notions of creativity, though, the kind of theological delight an integrated, artisanal theology promises must include both energies, if at different times. One's story lived outward into a covenantal community story, lived even further as participant of the Story of God, requires the discerning energies of "taking it apart." The articulation of one's theology puts the pieces back together, shaped for the purposes of sharing God's mercies, undying love, unexpected compassion.

Things we hold most sacred—our own lives, our conceptions of who God is and what is sacred—show the threat of expressive delight as well. One of my favorite icons shows Jesus with his head thrown back in a full-throated, embodied belly laugh. We only see him from the side, about shoulder height and above, but the visual association is one of a fully human guffaw. Now how do the words *guffaw* and *Jesus* sit side by side in your religious sensibilities? *Belly laugh* and *YHWH*? I love the icon because it clashes holy awe in God's otherness, sovereignty, and grace with an intimacy, light-heartedness, and enjoyment that dear friends share with one another. I confess Jesus' full humanity, so I am sure he laughed with his friends at least once or twice. The image continues to startle me into new awarenesses.

Jesus laughing with such abandon startles many practitioners of religious faith in their felt associations of God and humanity: the fear of God (which is the beginning of wisdom), invocation of God's presence, adoration and confession, conviction of human sin, humble repentance, unmerited salvation, imposed servanthood, self-sacrifice, lament, praise, liturgical celebration. These are all hefty terms for a life devoted to God and other. Yet expressive delight is no less important, perhaps even arguably more important, than all the solemnity we can muster. My father once told me that when God created the butterfly, She giggled. I love the jarring juxtaposition. Then there is Psalm 8: "O Lord, our Sovereign, how

2. Cameron, *Vein of Gold*, 127–28.
3. Ibid., 128.

majestic is your name in all the earth! You have set your glory above the heavens. Out of the mouths of babes and infants you have founded a bulwark . . ." Both/And. Utterly incomprehensible, unimaginable Presence and unexpectedly playful, imaginative Intimacy. Many of us in the governing worlds of theological education today lack the delight, in deference to the majesty.

This neglect presents a deeper challenge to communities of religious faith today, almost regardless of tradition. More than the confusion surrounding missions, or the polarized disputes about sexuality, or the wrestling with congregational identity. Those things are important and not to be underestimated, but they are less important than the receptive practices that open each and all of us to the best of human life that God intended from the beginning. Covenantal companionship that promises expressive, theological delight is perhaps the only antidote to the overwhelming fear, pain and suffering so prevalent in the world today. It is the seed, process, and blossom of a rooted and unending love, stronger than death. It lives an embodied trust into the world, with eyes wide open to even radical suffering, with hearts open wider in compassion. It signals a deep awareness and regret of one's own limitations, right alongside a sacred acceptance and redemption of them for ultimately creative purpose. It forms a careful stewardship of the least of us, open to the interdependent realities of shared nobody-ness between *us* and *them*.

Whatever else might be said, the aim here has been to nudge, encourage, and urge with practical observations a process that depends upon a willingness to enter into such covenant, to participate in it, to allow body-mind-spirit to be challenged, stretched, even threatened a little with grace beyond bounds. Intentional formation requires engagement with resources, persons, and theological institutions at a deeply intimate and risky level. Covenantal companionship presents the best, interpersonal, if risk-laden vehicle in which intentional formation in theological education can occur. Theologians will continue to offer the gift of hope examined and generations of traditions interpreted for a God known without Being in the name of undying love.[4] Covenantal companions will come alongside and mirror growth and grace.

Everything that precedes these pages is but preamble to the justice and mercy God intends for us all. Become reflective about companion-

4. Marion, *God Without Being*, 3–4.

ship. Take small risks in covenantal companionships that involve you in lived mission beyond your comfortable "communities." Look for the companions and rhythms that give you the most joy and are available to all. Then radically covenantal companionship begins, with a mutual recognition of being-claimed, by two or more people, each for the other, and by a Presence within and beyond any one of them. The routines, practices, or expressions vary infinitely, depending upon time, location, context, and participants' proclivities and stories. In contrast to popular religiosity and understandings of human will/power, there is no coercion, no authoritative interpretation, no technique, no manipulation, no seduction. The freedom of each participant to withdraw always remains. The seed of awareness is an invitation spurred by holy desire and an utter willingness to open to the calling, to be opened beyond polite, societal expectation. One must choose to open, or be opened, yet there is just as strong a sense of there being no other choice. Irresistible grace and the healing of hidden wounds occurs, but being claimed is not solely for that purpose. The purpose of being claimed is to serve one another on behalf of One and all. In order to learn limitations and to receive humility's gifts, one must receive such care from another. One must be open to being served as much as one desires to serve.

When disagreement arises—and it assuredly will, with great threat and wounding—the claim remains. Shared practice continues despite the difficulties. Deep listening is required, as well as a gentle tenacity to care for oneself amidst the call to serve the other's growth, as perceived within one's perspective, however frail, hurting, and limited it may be. Each participant deepens in ability to sustain the dissonances of ambiguity, felt-betrayal, and recovered trust. Each one grows stronger in resilience, deeper in self-awareness, and more regularly compassionate with one another and with all those one may encounter. As such, these companionships require sustenance and even regulation within broader covenantal companionship, webs of worship and practice that are crucial for living felt devotion outward, continually, in an ideologically polarized and intensely fearful public. The danger, otherwise, is an inwardness or relational narcissism with therefore misdirected charisms of faith, hoarded for "spiritual experience" instead of returned to the world so hungry for nourishment.

Most importantly, radically covenantal companionship promises a life of expressive delight and willing surrender undergirded by unpredictable but trustworthy practices of devotion and awakening. Life becomes luminous, vibrant, and recognizable, if beyond previous imagination. A deep sense begins to pervade continually deepening spiritual practices with intermittent and regular awareness: this sacred wholeness is on behalf of One and all, especially those most feared, rejected, angry, or disempowered within life's sufferings and grace.

Will the path articulated here be painless and easy? Of course not. Awakening is painful, which is why so few of us deepen practice enough to pursue it. Can the experts among us prepare us for the difficulties we will face? Not really. At least not those that will be the most important in shaping our spirits-minds-bodies for God's service. Will it be worth it, to risk into discomfort and receive gifts we had never imagined? Blessedly, assuredly so. Linda and Charles opened my eyes to the conundrum of faith and fragmentation that will face each of us whenever we attempt to deepen spiritual practice within a community or engage established traditions of faith within the worlds of theological education. Greater understandings of the difficulties—potential relationships of causes and effects—can help each of us make wiser decisions as we negotiate the conundrum. *A healthy* risk requires nothing less. Greater understanding will never reduce the felt-sensations of risk and vulnerability, however. Formation is never something we get right in practice or profession, but an ongoing process of waking up in public—intimate and vulnerable, recognizable and shared.

An artisanal theology—the traditionally inherited and embodied theology recognizable in delight and rooted in radically covenantal companionship—refuses to abandon anyone's ventured wisdom. It is steeped in the conviction that covenantal companionship will fire all voices into the deeper sustenance of mutual transformation. It is neither easy nor painless. But there is nothing so wondrous as a companionable delight on behalf of all. Might an irrepressible joy and an expressive delight be the whole point, simply too wonderful to dare to believe? Brother Roger of Taizé thought so: what you dare not hope for—that is precisely what the Spirit gives.[5]

5. Bourgeault, *Mystical Hope*, 1.

APPENDIX A: *Guidelines for Convening a Covenantal Group*

Convening a group toward covenantal community resembles an intuitive artistry much more than an informed, technical process. Several resources offer collaborative models, including professionally-supervisory approaches, congregational-team development, and less institutionally-located spirituality circles. A good online resource can be found at www.peerspirit.com, which introduces the sacred circle work of Christina Baldwin and Anne Linnea. It may be helpful to know from the start that I have begun this process several times, with widely varying senses of "success." It is a counter-cultural and humbling quest, but worthwhile in the end. Keep in mind your new and old learnings as you venture into such constructive communal endeavors. Some helpful resources:

Carnes, Robin Deen, and Sally Craig. *Sacred Circles: A Guide to Creating Your Own Women's Spirituality Group.* San Francisco: HarperSanFrancisco, 1999.
Cladis, George. *Leading the Team-Based Church.* San Francisco: Jossey-Bass, 1999.
Corey, Marianne Schneider, and Gerald Corey. *Groups: Process and Practice.* 5th edition. Pacific Grove, CA: Brooks/Cole, 1997; see especially, 105–33, "Forming a Group"

Those interested in finding participants for a fledgling group may consider all kinds of factors for who, where, what, when, how, and ultimately, why the group forms into a cohesive whole with potential for covenantal companionship(s).

- *Possible group composition* for enough familiarity to establish commonality of the group, yet enough diversity to provide ample opportunities for new perspectives, challenges, and intimacy based upon self-differentiation
- *The location for an initial group meeting*

- *The confidential character of a closed group* and *the advantages of an open group* during preliminary phases of group development

- *The covenantal character* of such a group

- *Possibly finding a partner, including early recruits in decision making*—exploring shared leadership from the start

The convener(s) and the forming group begin to chart their course, perhaps focusing on resources to be read and discussed, ultimately toward as much clarity as possible for the group's professed purpose and offering to its members, eventually, to the wider community. Some purposes and considerations are offered here.

- *A goal of presence and shared experience,* not agreement and/or comfort

- *A focus on spiritual development and communion with God* among peer fellowship

- *A formed intention of pastoral renewal for pastors by pastors*—and continual clarification of that hope

- *A discerned sharing of the word*—discriminating but plentiful conversation in search of

  » Psychologically stable people, invited out of true interest and not any 'should' or 'ought to' mentality

  » Different kinds of people

  » Enough interested possibilities to end up with 5-8 committed members

- *Need for honesty and self-disclosure*

- *Need for acknowledgment of one's shadow, frailty, limitations, alongside celebrations and offers of grace, advocacy and compassion*

- *Need for acknowledgment of sin*

A good way to begin is simply to gather a "pre-group" meeting with persons who have expressed interest or responded to an invitation to consider joining a covenantal group. I suggest a lay-leader or trained facilitator will serve best for this purpose, in contrast to a congregational pastor. Pastoral support—explicit or implicit—is quite necessary for any larger community initiatives of group development, but for obvious reasons given in previous chapters, pastors themselves struggle with group dynamics and healthy participation just as much as the next person. Such a pre-group gathering might be focused with the following considerations:

- *Council sharing*: one person at a time takes a turn speaking while the others listen
  - » No interruptions
  - » Only how YOU feel, not how others feel or should feel etc.
- *Listening without an agenda*—open to new thoughts/feelings and not about being in agreement. This is about being present.
- *Shared ownership*
- *Confidentiality*—trust first, then risk-taking and then intimacy
- *Taking responsibility for one's own needs*
  - » Members will ask for what they themselves need, not expecting the group to know that already and provide
- *Self-reflection*—must step back and observe group functioning; any facilitator will help
- *Focus on spiritual development and renewal*
- *Commitment*—shared intention and commitment increases success/health of group
  - » Allow sufficient time, practice patience and discernment if an obviously cohesive group does not form easily. It may *not* form, which is okay, if not desirable.

Each fledgling group may also articulate a verbal and/or written covenant by which participants understand and live out their covenantal commitment to one another. It is advisable **to be specific** about appropriate behaviors and expectations for "committed group participation." Be sure to define "voluntary" and "involuntary" absences. See George Cladis' *Leading the Team Based Church* for a sample team covenant. Good things to remember include:

- Review and/or revise group covenant—verbal or written—once or twice a year
- Orient any new team members to the covenant

- Remember covenantal intentions by keeping a copy in a visible but protected space

Finding a group facilitator—usually a pastoral counselor, spiritual director, or professional with training in group dynamics—offers the most structured and safest approach to a fledgling companionship whose aim is to enter into the vulnerable space of covenantal or radically covenantal companionship. The fee-for-service for this preliminary investment can be divided between the group's members such that cost does not become prohibitive.

APPENDIX B: *Creating a Spiritual Autobiography*

A spiritual autobiography is more than any 4–5 page document (or project) you create. The entire process of composing your spiritual autobiography is summarized in various resources. See, for example, Richard Peace, *Spiritual Autobiography: Discovering and Sharing Your Spiritual Story*. A spiritual autobiography actually begins with picking a date on which you will share your story with your covenantal companions. Deadlines encourage discipline like little else. The process continues as you are invited to read resources and to awaken to your life story in new and unexpected ways. You will describe it first to yourself in notes and/or a manuscript, then with others in your group. Several things to remember:

1. There is no way to summarize your life in the 20–25 minutes you will have in any group's process, therefore the point is to examine and learn, examine and learn, examine and learn . . .

2. You know less about yourself now than you will when you have shared your story. If you are willing to risk becoming more aware of the mystery of being human and a child of God, you will come to hear unexpected elements of your own story, both desirable and undesirable things. If you are not willing, then you will complete an exercise with little gain for yourself or others.

3. Others have done this before you and even survived. Others will do it after you have finished. Any anxiety or apprehension is normal.

Basic process:

Write[1] a 4–5 page (1.5 spaced, at most) spiritual autobiography to share with your group. The process begins now, and the assignment begins now.

1. There are other media in which to tell your story, of course, if you have access

111

1. Pray for God's guidance, for what you are to learn and what will form your own discipleship in new and creative ways.

2. Divide your life into various periods of time and examine each for high points, low points, outcomes of growth (intellectual, emotional, behavioral, relational, growth in service).

3. Describe each period in writing or pictures, either in notes, or with a manuscript, or even in a collage of magazine cut-outs.

4. Time yourself as you practice telling your story, presenting the project you have compiled as you anticipate sharing it with a group of companions. (A page of 1.5 spaced text should take 3–4 minutes to read, for instance).

5. Edit or alter your presentation for time sensitivity in your group.

Remember: you are only sharing pivotal moments in your life and the details that have led up to them, as you have discerned. *You are not summarizing who you are*—an impossible task. You are learning from your own story both how you understand yourself, and what others can see in your story that you cannot.

The sharing of your story should take no more than 20–25 minutes, to allow for feedback in the remaining time (up to an hour) from members of your group. This means *no more than* 5 pages of manuscript, normal 12-point font, and *no less than* 4 pages, normal 12-point font. The feedback from your group is to accomplish 4 things:

1. To give you insight and perspective on your life that only others can give.

2. To name the strengths that they see in your life and how they have made you who you are.

3. To name the "growing edges" or challenges through which spiritual maturity will grow in personal and any professional pursuits, at least if you attend to them with care and intention.

4. To celebrate who God has made you to be, at this time in your life.

---

to the resources: audio, video, podcast, and more. Confirm and explore this with your group as you all see fit.

APPENDIX C: *Creating a Case Study for Teaching/Learning*

INTRODUCTION

What is a case study? One of several ways of doing social science research (others include experiments, surveys, histories, and analysis of archival information). Type of investigation determined by (a) the type of research question, (b) the control an investigator has over actual behavioral events, and (c) the focus on contemporary as opposed to historical phenomena.

Case studies are the preferred strategy of inquiry when

1. "How" or "why" questions are being posed,

2. The investigator has little control over events, and

3. The focus is on a contemporary phenomenon within some real-life context.[1]

General flow of process/practice to come:

Description: What descriptive information is relevant toward deepening your own (and others') understanding? Get as accurate a sense of the critical incident or ministry event as you are able: context, time, participants, pre-history and post-history to the interaction, observations—not interpretations yet!

Evaluation: What do you perceive as the core issues at play—your own, systemic, interaction between them? Your initial critical question usually arises here. Presenters name their critical question and write it at the top of their report.

1. Yin, *Case Study Research*, 1–18.

Analysis: What alternative possibilities emerge for "what happened"? This stage intends to remove any obstacles and find among alternative possibilities the one that seems most viable for continued ministry in the situation.

Theological naming: Where is God in the conversation, interaction, event? Hint: God isn't always the comforter or felt "good" in the interaction.

Discernment: Given a renewed examination of this event, what may be a viable response within the ministry situation? What is a faithful "next step"?

PROCESS/PRACTICE—PREPARATIONS TO CONCLUSION

Case study investigations involve a *critical reflection process* designed to develop *critical thinking skills* and *self-awareness* within your ongoing intentional formation and your discernment of gifts for ministry (regardless of specific "calling" or "vocation"). The two areas of focus should be your *own preparations/examination of the event,* and *the presentation of the case-study report* with your covenantal group.

Preparation

1. **Choose a conversation, interaction, or interpersonal event from your ministry experience.** Reflect on your experiences of the last 6 months or so; take at least 15–20 minutes of *undistracted time* to engage this process. Select (from any images or memories that come to mind) a conversation, personal interaction, or interpersonal event that created an emotive response in you—either positive or negative. The emotive response is the clue that something deeper was touched and deserves further examination in a supportive and challenging community designed to help you gain critical perspective and become aware of your own part in ministry formation.

2. **Write the event in a "case-study" report (up to 3 pages, single-spaced).** In no more than three pages (single-spaced) represent the interaction in print—changing the names of any participants

in it (except yourself, of course). Confidentiality requires protection of any other participants' names.

3. **Verbatim portion.** If it is a conversation, offer a reconstruction of the conversation verbatim: print what you said as the "event" began, followed by what s/he said, followed by what you responded etc. . . . until a feasible ending. This verbatim conversation is part of the report but should not be longer than one page. If the interaction is not primarily a conversation, describe it in as much detail as you can: context, participants, specific setting, time of day, pre-history to the event, any post-history to the interaction. Paint as much of the picture of the interaction as you are able, within a brief report format.

The covenant group conversation will progress through phases of description, evaluation, analysis, theological dimensions, and mutual discernment. The remainder of the case study report should offer your own, initial understanding of the event as you have evaluated, analyzed, and discerned meaning and action within it. *Your next step of preparation for the peer-group conversation is to name your critical question about which you hope to learn, teach.* **Write this question at the very top of your case study report.**

Make one copy of the typed report for each companion and facilitator, if one is a part of your group's process.

Presentation of report at peer-group

1. **Present the report by reading it aloud.**

   Bring copies of this report—one for each peer and your facilitator—and present the report by reading it aloud. Any verbatim dialogues should be recreated with the reading support of a peer or two.

2. **Participate in a conversation of mutual discernment with your peers and your facilitator.**

   Your group will engage you in a critically reflective and discerning conversation about your interaction and your case-study report of it. The phases of the process—the initial process which you have engaged in order to prepare for the presentation—have been described above. Your conversation should progress through these various stages, concluding with a mutual discernment of responsible action or "next steps" for the event examined. *One helpful logistic tip*: assign a peer who is not presenting to be time-keeper responsible for alerting the group to its own timely progress through *all* the stages—10–15 minutes for you to present, 30–40 minutes to discuss. Use your time wisely!

Description

Evaluation

Analysis

Interpretation - Theological Naming

Discernment of action/"next step"

CONCLUSION

Conclude your own learning/teaching from the process by articulating what your critical question is *now*, after the conversation. *Write it at the bottom of your case-study report.* File case-study report in a safe place for continuing review. Honor your own participation in the process: if it was difficult, find another supportive place in which to debrief about it; if it was emotionally powerful in some way, celebrate the opportunity to have engaged in The Process.

APPENDIX D: *More Guidelines for Creating*
a Theological Statement

A theological statement for ministry is an opportunity for integrative thinking and careful articulation of your theological formation up to this moment. It is simply a *working* document, not (as often popularly conceived) the culmination of your faith or understanding of God and God's mission within this world. Such a statement offers opportunity

- to articulate a critically, theologically informed stance on God, World, Church, Mission, and Leadership (ordained and lay)
- to identify the theological tradition in which you have been formed and/or are being formed
  - denominational (for Board or certification purposes, toward ordained ministry)
  - descriptive (Reformed, process, liberationist, et al)
  - declared/defined (conceptual coherence and clarity of important themes)
- to be brief but personally pithy: 12–15 pages in length, 12-point font, double-spaced, 1″ margins.

Process Highlights:

1. Considering classical and contemporary theological voices offers opportunity to reflect somewhat systematically on the function of scripture, reason, tradition, and experience in your critical theological understanding.

2. Helpful structure for your reflections can be found in both the Apostles' Creed and the Nicene Creed. Read each of these through

117

several times, noting structure and phrases that resonate and those that you struggle to understand or profess in contemporary language.

3. Denominational documents also offer substantial guidance on requirements and considerations for entering (ordained) ministry through critical theological development.

> United Methodist Church reads the *Book of Discipline* (esp. ¶¶ 101–4, ¶¶ 301–69 for understandings of theological task and ordained ministry, ¶¶ 120–41 for church and leadership);

> Presbyterian Church (USA) reads their Constitution, the *Book of Confessions* and the *Book of Order* (esp. G-6.0000–6.0500 and G-14.0000–14.0800 for understanding theological task and ordained ministry, G-1.0000–G-6.0500 for church and leadership/membership).

> United Church of Christ reads the UCC Manual on Ministry, particularly section 3 of 10, (http://www.ucc.org/ministers/manual/MOM%2003%20Ordained.pdf).

> Baptist (ABC) students, see http://www.ministerscouncil .com/FAQ.aspx for proper avenues into local and regional requirements for theological task and pursuit of ordained ministry.

> Church of the Brethren students, see http://www.brethren .org/genbd/ministry/index.htm for denominational process and understandings of theological task.

4. Return to your favorite and difficult theology texts and resources, or other theological-historical contributions to your current understanding. Review Chapter Four and begin to jot down the various questions you have wrestled with or heard. Make a list of scriptural books and/or letters (*not* verses! Proof-texting suggests fear, not reflection or a faithful curiosity) that have spoken to you in your faith journey.

5. Write your first draft, however you write best—outline, jump in and rely on stream-of-consciousness flow, write summary paragraphs of your questions and descriptions of God, World, Church, Mission, Leadership. See Chapter Five. The preliminary

draft to share with your companions must also weave supportive and challenging commentary from these scriptural and theological voices you have encountered.

6. *At least 10–15 citations from the biblical witness* (both that support your stance and that contradict/challenge your point of view—showing your awareness of complexity and need for critical interpretation of sources), *and from authors from historical and contemporary theological discourse* (Paul, Church Fathers and Mothers, mystics or visionaries, Reformers such as Calvin, Luther, or Zwingli, Wesley or Knox, contemporary voices such as Ty Inbody, Daniel Migliore, Serene Jones, William Placher, Wendy Farley, Catherine LaCugna—just to name a few). *These must be properly cited.*[1]

7. Your presentation of this theological statement for ministry will require (1) copies provided for each group member, and (2) your choosing 2–4 sections about which you would like commentary or contribution. Choose sections which you feel *least* prepared on, in order to receive most benefit. Read through these sections aloud and then participate in the supervisory discernment conversation. Edit and revise the statement afterwards, as per contributions gained.

1. Vyhmeister, *Quality Research Papers for Students of Religion and Theology*, 7–13, 32–39, 62–81.

Bibliography

Addison, Howard A., and Barbara Eve Breitman. *Jewish Spiritual Direction: an Innovative Guide from Tradition and Contemporary Sources.* Woodstock, VT: Jewish Lights, 2006.

Aelred of Rievaulx. *Spiritual Friendship.* Translated by Mary Eugenia Laker SSND. Cistercian Fathers Series Number Five. Kalamazoo, MI: Cistercian, 1974.

Ammerman, Nancy T. *Congregation and Community.* New Brunswick, NJ: Rutgers University Press, 2001.

Anderson, Herbert and Edward Foley. *Mighty Stories, Dangerous Rituals: Weaving Together the Human and the Divine.* San Francisco: Jossey-Bass, 1998.

Anderson, Ray S. *An Emergent Theology for Emerging Churches.* Downers Grove, IL: InterVarsity, 2006.

Barth, Karl. *Church Dogmatics.* II/2: The Doctrine of God. Edited by G.W. Bromiley and T. F. Torrance. Edinburgh: T. & T. Clark, 1977.

———. *Church Dogmatics.* III/2: The Doctrine of God. Edited by G. W. Bromiley and T. F. Torrance. Edinburgh: T. & T. Clark, 1977.

———. *Karl Barth: Theologian of Freedom.* The Making of Modern Theology Series. Edited by Clifford Green. Minneapolis, MN: Fortress, 1991.

Bass, Dorothy C., editor. *Practicing Our Faith: A Way of Life for a Seeking People.* San Francisco: Jossey-Bass, 1997.

Bass, Dorothy C., and Craig Dykstra, editors. *For Life Abundant: Practical Theology, Theological Education, and Christian Ministry.* Grand Rapids: Eerdmans, 2008.

Bass, Dorothy C., and Don C. Richter. *Way to Live: Christian Practices for Teens.* Nashville, TN: Upper Room, 2002.

Belenky, Mary, Blythe Clinchy, Nancy Goldberger, and Jill Tarule. *Women's Ways of Knowing: The Development of Self, Voice, and Mind.* San Francisco: HarperCollins, 1987.

Bell, John L. *He Was In the World: Meditations for Public Worship.* Chicago: GIA, 1995.

Berryman, Jerome W. *Godly Play: An Imaginative Approach to Religious Education.* Minneapolis, MN: Augsburg, 1995.

Pope Benedict XVI, and Henry Taylor. *Truth and Tolerance: Christian Belief and World Religions.* San Francisco: Ignatius, 2004.

Bernstein, Richard J. *Beyond Objectivism and Relativism: Science, Hermeneutics, and Praxis.* Philadelphia: University of Pennsylvania Press, 1983.

Bondi, Roberta C. *Memories of God: Theological Reflections on a Life.* Nashville, TN: Abingdon, 1995.

———. *To Love as God Loves: Conversations with the Early Church.* Philadelphia: Fortress, 1987.

Bourdieu, Pierre. *Outline of a Theory of Practice.* Translated by Richard Nice. Cambridge: Cambridge University Press, 1977.

Bourgeault, Cynthia. *Mystical Hope: Trusting in the Mercy of God.* New York: Cowley, 2001.

———. *The Wisdom Way of Knowing: Reclaiming an Ancient Tradition for Awakening the Heart.* San Francisco: Jossey-Bass, 2003.

Browning, Don S. *A Fundamental Practical Theology: Descriptive and Strategic Proposals.* Minneapolis, MN: Augsburg Fortress, 1996.

Brueggemann, Walter. *Finally Comes the Poet: Daring Speech for Proclamation.* Minneapolis, MN: Fortress, 1989.

———. *Theology of the Old Testament.* Minneapolis: Fortress, 1997.

Butler Bass, Diana. *The Practicing Congregation: Imagining a New Old Church.* Herndon, VA: Alban Institute, 2004.

Calvin, John. *Institutes of the Christian Religion.* Edited by John T. McNeill. Translated by Ford Lewis Battles. Philadelphia: Westminster, 1960.

Cameron, Julia. *The Artist's Way: a Spiritual Path to Higher Creativity.* New York: Tarcher/Putnam, 1992.

———. *The Vein of Gold: a Journey to Your Creative Heart.* New York: Tarcher/Putnam, 1996.

Carroll, Jackson. *As One Without Authority: Reflective Leadership in Ministry.* Louisville, KY: Westminster John Knox, 1991.

———. *God's Potters: Pastoral Leadership and the Shaping of Congregations.* Grand Rapids: Eerdmans, 2006.

———. "The Professional Model of Ministry: Is it Worth Saving?" *Theological Education* 21:2 (1985) 7–48.

Carroll, Jackson, Barbara G. Wheeler, Daniel O. Aleshire, and Penny Long Marler. *Being There: Culture and Formation in Two Theological Schools.* New York: Oxford University Press, 1997.

Corbitt, J. Nathan, and Vivian Nix-Early. *Taking It to the Streets: Using the Arts to Transform your Community.* Grand Rapids: Baker, 2003.

Craddock, Fred B. *Overhearing the Gospel.* St. Louis: Chalice, 2002.

———. "A Rare Rhetorical Performance," "In the Service of the Gospel," "For Those Who Need to Hear it Again." McCord Public Lecture Series. Princeton, NJ: Princeton Theological Seminary, October 14–16, 1996.

Davies, Robertson. *The Rebel Angels*. New York: Penguin, 1983.

Dawn, Marva J. *Keeping the Sabbath Wholly: Ceasing, Resting, Embracing, Feasting*. Grand Rapids: Eerdmans, 1989.

———. *The Sense of the Call: A Sabbath Way of Life for Those Who Serve God, the Church, and the World*. Grand Rapids: Eerdmans, 2006.

Dorje, Rig'dzin. *Dangerous Friend: the Teacher-Student Relationship in Vajrayana Buddhism*. Boston: Shambhala, 2001.

Dykstra, Craig. *Growing in Faith: Education and Christian Practices*. Louisville, KY: Geneva, 1999.

———. "Reconceiving Practice." In *Shifting Boundaries: Contextual Approaches to the Structure of Theological Education*. Edited by Barbara G. Wheeler and Edward Farley. Louisville, KY: Westminster John Knox, 1991.

Eisner, Elliot W. *The Educational Imagination: On the Design and Evaluation of School Programs*. Third edition. New York: Macmillan, 1994.

Engelmann, Kim V. *Running in Circles: How False Spirituality Traps Us in Unhealthy Relationships*. Downers Grove, IL: InterVarsity, 2007.

Erikson, Erik. *Identity and the Life Cycle*. New York: Norton, 1980.

Farley, Edward. *Practicing Gospel: Unconventional Thoughts on the Church's Ministry*. Louisville, KY: Westminster John Knox, 2003.

———. *Theologia: the Fragmentation and Unity of Theological Education*. Philadelphia: Fortress, 1983.

Foster, Charles R., Lisa E. Dahill, Lawrence A. Goleman, and Barbara Wang Tolentino. *Educating Clergy: Teaching Practices and Pastoral Imagination*. Preparation for the Professions Series. Stanford, CA: Carnegie Foundation for the Advancement of Teaching/Jossey-Bass, 2006.

Fowler, Floyd J. *Survey Research Methods*. 3rd ed. Applied Social Research Methods Series. Thousand Oaks, CA: Sage, 2001.

Freire, Paulo. *Pedagogy of the Oppressed*. Translated by Myra Bergman Ramos. Revised twentieth-anniversary edition. New York: Continuum, 1993.

Gardner, Howard. *The Unschooled Mind: How Children Think and Schools Should Teach*. San Francisco: HarperCollins, 1991.

Gilligan, Carol. *In a Different Voice: Psychological Theory and Women's Development*. Cambridge, MA: Harvard University Press, 1993.

Goldberg, Natalie. *Long Quiet Highway: Waking Up in America*. New York: Bantam, 1994.

Granovetter, Mark S. "The Strength of Weak Ties" *American Journal of Sociology* 78 (1973) 1360–80.

Grenz, Stanley. *A Primer on Post-Modernism*. Grand Rapids: Eerdmans, 1996.

Hauerwas, Stanley. "A Story-Formed Community: Reflections on *Watership Down.*" In *The Hauerwas Reader*, edited by John Berkman and Michael Cartwright, 171–99. Durham, NC: Duke University Press, 2001.

Hauerwas, Stanley, and L. Gregory Jones, editors. *Why Narrative? Readings in Narrative Theology.* Grand Rapids: Eerdmans, 1997.

Hawkins, Thomas R. *The Learning Congregation: A New Vision of Leadership.* Louisville, KY: Westminster John Knox, 1997.

Hess, Lisa M. "Formation in the Worlds of Theological Education: Moving From What to How." *Teaching Theology and Religion* 11 (2008) 14–23.

———. "Sabbath Renewal: Recovering Play in Pastoral Ministry." *The Clergy Journal* 81 (2004) 15–16.

Hilsman, Gordon J. *Intimate Spirituality: the Catholic Way of Love and Sex.* New York: Rowman & Littlefield, 2007.

Holland, Dorothy, William Lachicotte Jr., Debra Skinner, and Carole Cain, *Identity and Agency in Cultural Worlds.* Cambridge, MA: Harvard University Press, 1998.

Jackson, Michael. *The Politics of Storytelling: Violence, Transgression, and Intersubjectivity.* Copenhagen: Museum Tusculanum Press/University of Copenhagen, 2006.

Johnson, Robert A. *Owning Your Own Shadow: Understanding the Dark Side of the Psyche.* San Francisco: HarperSanFranciso, 1991.

Jones, W. Paul. *Worlds Within a Congregation: Dealing with Theological Diversity.* Nashville, TN: Abingdon, 2000.

Justes, Emma J. *Hearing Beyond the Words: How to Become a Listening Pastor.* Nashville, TN: Abingdon, 2006.

Keating, Thomas. *The Human Condition: Contemplation and Transformation.* Mahwah, NJ: Paulist, 1999.

Kelsey, David H. *Uses of Scripture in Recent Theology.* Philadelphia: Fortress, 1975.

Kimball, Dan. *The Emerging Church.* Grand Rapids: Zondervan, 2003.

Klimoski, Victor. "The Evolving Dynamics of Formation." In *Practical Wisdom on Theological Teaching and Learning*, edited by Malcolm L. Warford. New York: Peter Lang, 2005.

Koppel, Michael S. "A Pastoral Theological Reflection on Play in the Ministry." *Journal of Pastoral Theology* 13 (2003) 3–12.

Kula, Irwin, with Linda Loewenthal. *Yearnings: Embracing the Sacred Messiness of Life.* New York: Hyperion, 2006.

Lehman, Paul L. *Ethics in a Christian Context.* Eugene, OR: Wipf & Stock, 1998.

Loder, James E. *The Transforming Moment.* 2nd ed. Colorado Springs, CO: Helmers & Howard, 1989.

———. *The Logic of the Spirit: Human Development in Theological Perspective.* San Francisco: Jossey-Bass, 1998.

Loder, James E., and W. Jim Neidhardt, *The Knight's Move: the Relational Logic of the Spirit in Science and Theology*. Colorado Springs, CO: Helmers & Howard, 1992.

Macek, Ellen A. "Advice Manuals and the Formation of English Protestant and Catholic Clerical Identities 1560–1660." *Nederlands Archief voor Kerkgeschiedenis* 85 (2005) 315–31.

MacIntyre, Alasdair. *After Virtue: A Study in Moral Theory*. 2nd ed. Notre Dame, IN: University of Notre Dame Press, 1984.

Marion, Jean-Luc. *The Erotic Phenomenon*. Chicago: University of Chicago Press, 2006.

———. *God Without Being*. Translated by Thomas A. Carlson. Chicago: University of Chicago Press, 1991.

May, Gerald. *Will and Spirit*. San Francisco: HarperSanFrancisco, 1982.

McGrath, Alister E. *Christian Theology: An Introduction*. 3rd edition. Malden, MA: Blackwell, 2001.

McKim, Donald K. *Introducing the Reformed Faith: Biblical Revelation, Christian Tradition, Contemporary Significance*. Louisville, KY: Westminster John Knox, 2001.

Merton, Thomas. *No Man Is an Island*. New York: Barnes & Noble, 2005.

———. *Thomas Merton Spiritual Master: Essential Writings*. Edited by Lawrence S. Cunningham. Mahweh, NJ: Paulist, 1992.

Migliore, Daniel L. *Faith Seeking Understanding: An Introduction to Christian Theology*. Grand Rapids: Eerdmans, 1991.

Miller, Vincent J. *Consuming Religion: Christian Faith and Practice in a Consumer Culture*. New York: Continuum, 2004.

Morgan, Richard Lyon. *Remembering Your Story: Creating Your Own Spiritual Autobiography*. Nashville, TN: Upper Room, 2002.

Morse, Christopher. *Not Every Spirit: A Dogmatics of Christian Disbelief*. Harrisburg, PA: Trinity, 1994.

Myers, Ken. "Joy May End in Grief: Re-Imagining Leisure in the Face of Relentless Entertainment." Sound recording. North Cincinnati Community Church, Cincinnati, Ohio. October 3–5, 2003.

Palmer, Parker. *To Know As We Are Known: Education as a Spiritual Journey*. San Francisco: HarperSanFrancisco, 1993.

Pannenberg, Wolfhart. *Anthropology in Theological Perspective*. Translated by Matthew J. O'Connell. Philadelphia: Westminster, 1985.

Peace, Richard. *Spiritual Autobiography: Discovering and Sharing Your Spiritual Story*. Colorado Springs, CO: NavPress, 1998.

Placher, William C., and David Willis-Watkins, *Belonging to God: A Commentary on A Brief Statement of Faith*. Louisville, KY: Westminster John Knox, 1992.

Ploeger, Albert K. *Dare We Observe? The Importance of Art Works for Consciousness of Diakonia in (Post-)modern Church.* Leuven: Peeters, 2002.

Pohly, Kenneth. *Transforming the Rough Places: The Ministry of Supervision.* 2nd ed. Franklin, TN: Providence House, 2001.

Polanyi, Michael. *Personal Knowledge: Towards a Post-Critical Philosophy.* Chicago: University of Chicago Press, 1962.

Powers, Elizabeth, and Amy Mandelker, editors. *Pilgrim Souls: A Collection of Spiritual Autobiography.* New York: Touchstone, 1999.

Presbyterian Church (USA). *The Book of Confessions.* Louisville, KY: Westminster John Knox, 1999.

Prothero, Stephen. *Religious Literacy: What Every American Needs to Know—and Doesn't.* San Francisco: HarperOne, 2007.

Putnam, Robert. *Bowling Alone: The Collapse and Revival of American Community.* New York: Touchstone, 2000.

Reinhart, Peter. *Bread Upon the Waters: a Pilgrimage toward Self-Discovery and Spiritual Truth.* Cambridge: Perseus, 2000.

———. *Brother Juniper's Bread Book: Slow Rise as Method and Metaphor.* Cambridge: Perseus, 1991.

Reno, R. R. *In the Ruins of the Church: Sustaining Faith in an Age of Diminished Christianity.* Grand Rapids: Brazos, 2003.

Rumi, Jelaluddin. *The Glance: Songs of Soul-Meeting.* Translated by Coleman Barks with Nevit Ergin. New York: Viking, 1999.

Sayers, Dorothy. *The Mind of the Maker.* Westport, CT: Greenwood, 1941.

Schnarch, David. *Passionate Marriage: Keeping Love and Intimacy Alive in Committed Relationships* Farmingdale, NY: Owl, 1998.

Schneiders, Sandra M. "Approaches to the Study of Christian Spirituality." In *The Blackwell Companion to Christian Spirituality*, ed. Arthur Holder. Malden, MA: Blackwell, 2005.

Schüssler Fiorenza, Elisabeth. *Bread Not Stone: the Challenge of Feminist Biblical Interpretation.* 10th ann. ed. Boston: Beacon, 1995.

Soelle, Dorothee. *Theology for Skeptics: Reflections on God.* Minneapolis, MN: Fortress, 1995.

Steiner, George. *Real Presences.* Chicago: University of Chicago Press, 1989.

Spong, John Shelby. *Why Christianity Must Change or Die: A Bishop Speaks to Believers in Exile.* San Francisco: HarperSanFranciso, 1998.

Stone, Howard W., and James O. Duke. *How to Think Theologically.* Minneapolis, MN: Fortress, 2006.

Subhuti with Subhamati. *Buddhism and Friendship.* Moseley, Birmingham, UK: Windhorse, 2004.

Volf, Miroslav. *Exclusion and Embrace: a Theological Exploration of Identity, Otherness, and Reconciliation.* Nashville, TN: Abingdon, 1996.

Volf, Miroslav, and Dorothy Bass, editors. *Practicing Theology: Beliefs and Practices in Christian Life.* Grand Rapids: Eerdmans, 2002.

Vyhmeister, Nancey Jean. *Quality Research Papers for Students of Religion and Theology.* Grand Rapids: Zondervan, 2001.

Wakefield, Dan. *The Story of Your Life: Writing a Spiritual Autobiography.* Boston: Beacon, 1990.

Warford, Malcolm L., editor. *Practical Wisdom: On Theological Teaching and Learning.* New York: Peter Lang, 2005.

Warren, Rick. *The Purpose-Driven Church.* Grand Rapids: Zondervan, 1995.

Weaver, Andrew J., and Donald E. Messer. *Connected Spirits: Friends and Spiritual Journeys.* Cleveland, OH: Pilgrim, 2007.

Wheeler, Barbara G. "Strangers: A Dialogue about the Church," New York Avenue Presbyterian Church, Washington D.C., November 7, 2003.

Williamson, Marianne. *A Return to Love: Reflections on the Principles of A Course in Miracles.* San Francisco: Harper Collins, 1992.

Willimon, William H. *Pastor: A Reader for Ordained Ministry.* Nashville, TN: Abingdon, 2002.

———. *Pastor: The Theology and Practice of Ordained Ministry.* Nashville, TN: Abingdon, 2002.

Wimberly, Anne Streaty, and Evelyn L. Parker. *In Search of Wisdom: Faith Formation in the Black Church.* Nashville, TN: Abingdon, 2003.

Wogaman, J. Philip. *Faith and Fragmentation: Reflections on the Future of Christianity.* Louisville, KY: Westminster John Knox, 2004.

Yin, Robert K. *Case-Study Research: Designs and Methods.* Applied Social Research Methods Series 5. Thousand Oaks, CA: Sage, 2002.

Lightning Source UK Ltd.
Milton Keynes UK
UKHW010101170819
348104UK00004B/1135/P